For Deuce,

Praise for the Prior Edition of *Disrupt*

"*Disrupt* is a simple yet incredibly powerful thought process that can help turn your business upside-down in seconds. Are you prepared to DISRUPT your business?"

—**Martin Lindstrom**, best-selling author of *Buyology*

"Remember the old Apple tagline, urging us all to 'Think Different'? In this book, Luke Williams shows us how to do precisely that. *Disrupt* helps you look at business—and the world around you—through a fresh lens, one that turns assumptions and convention upside down. Best of all, this is a practical book for the real world—Williams reveals not just how to come up with disruptive ideas, but how to nurture them, test them, pitch them, and ultimately make them real and profitable."

—**Warren Berger**, author of *A More Beautiful Question: The Power of Inquiry to Spark Breakthrough Ideas*

"Luke Williams has a powerful message for companies today: Don't wait for a couple guys in a garage to come up with an idea that will upend your business. With the tools he outlines in *Disrupt*, companies can light their own innovative sparks, ensuring that they will be their industry's pacesetters, instead of the ones left in the dust."

—**Linda Tischler**, Senior Editor, *Fast Company*

"If you need to drive disruptive innovation in your own organization—and you do—this is the guide you've been looking for. Luke Williams not only knows what it takes to create disruptive innovation. He knows how to explain it, in simple, clear, and practical concepts that anyone can use in their own organization. Buy this book if you want your work to make a difference."

—**David L. Rogers**, executive director of the Center on Global Brand Leadership, and author of *The Network Is Your Customer: Five Strategies to Thrive in a Digital Age*

"With its examples of game-changing disruptions, *Disrupt* is an essential read. This very practical step-by-step guide will enable you to successfully implement the 'think different' imperative."

—**Stewart Emery**, best-selling co-author of *Success Built to Last* and *Do you Matter? How Great Design Will Make People Love Your Company*

"Luke teaches us that the 'best' in best practice is to approach a business with no fear and new eyes."

—**Scott Galloway**, Professor of Marketing, NYU Stern; Founder, L2

"Luke Williams is the master at unleashing big thoughts. His book, *Disrupt*, shows us how to do what sometimes seems impossible— conceiving and executing bold ideas with massive potential. At the Nike Foundation, we've put Luke's principles to work and had tremendous results."

—**Stuart Hogue**, Director, Systems at Scale, Nike Foundation

"A truly timely book, *Disrupt* has the power to change the world for many of us by uncovering the act of innovative disruption necessary to keep evolving in the years to come."

—**Ric Peralta**, CEO, ATTIK

"The game has changed; to thrive and not just survive, companies need to shake up the status quo and be disruptive."

—**Bill Wackermann**, author of *Flip the Script*

"For those companies second-guessing their future paths, ponder no longer. *Disrupt* provides that path, and it may be your only real strategy in today's climate."

—**Andy Stefanovich**, Chief Curator and Provocateur, Prophet

"At some time, someone somewhere is going to disrupt your entire industry. Shouldn't it be you? In this easy-to-follow step-by-step guide, Luke Williams reveals a way of thinking that has the power to transform your business. Read this book before your competitors do."

—**Cordell Ratzlaff**, Director of User-Centered Design, Cisco

"I've observed Luke's process of disruptive thinking generate remarkably innovative solutions. I hope that many more companies will disrupt their existing innovation processes to benefit as well. They'll be glad they did!"

—**Peter N. Golder**, Professor of Marketing, Tuck School of Business at Dartmouth, and co-author of *Will and Vision: How Latecomers Grow to Dominate Markets*

Disrupt

Think the Unthinkable to Spark Transformation in Your Business

Second Edition

Luke Williams

Publisher: Paul Boger
Editor-in-Chief: Amy Neidlinger
Executive Editor: Jeanne Levine
Cover Designer: Drive Communications
Managing Editor: Kristy Hart
Project Editor: Lori Lyons
Proofreader: Katie Matejka
Senior Indexer: Cheryl Lenser
Senior Compositor: Gloria Schurick
Manufacturing Buyer: Dan Uhrig
Illustrations: Luke Williams

© 2016 by Luke Williams
Publishing as Pearson Education, Inc.

Old Tappan, New Jersey 07675

For information about buying this title in bulk quantities, or for special sales opportunities (which may include electronic versions; custom cover designs; and content particular to your business, training goals, marketing focus, or branding interests), please contact our corporate sales department at corpsales@pearsoned.com or (800) 382-3419.

For government sales inquiries, please contact governmentsales@pearsoned.com.

For questions about sales outside the U.S., please contact international@pearsoned.com.

Company and product names mentioned herein are the trademarks or registered trademarks of their respective owners.

Psycho shower image: Paramount Pictures/Hulton Archive/Getty Images

Printed in the United States of America

4   17

ISBN-10: 0-13-399590-9
ISBN-13: 978-0-13-399590-9

Pearson Education LTD.
Pearson Education Australia PTY, Limited.
Pearson Education Singapore, Pte. Ltd.
Pearson Education North Asia, Ltd.
Pearson Education Canada, Ltd.
Pearson Educación de Mexico, S.A. de C.V.
Pearson Education—Japan
Pearson Education Malaysia, Pte. Ltd.

Library of Congress Control Number: 2015943784

For my parents

Contents

PART III: The Disruptive Leader

Notes about Second Edition

In the four years since the first edition of Disrupt was published, I've had numerous discussions with managers, consultants, and educators across a diverse range of industries. And one request that I heard a lot was to go deeper into the leadership aspects of disruptive thinking. To address those suggestions, I've added a preface and a new section—Part III—that are designed to do exactly that.

Please keep in mind, though, as you read this section, that the ideas I'll be discussing are intended only to encourage you to develop your own ways of thinking about, managing, and leading innovation.

PREFACE TO THE SECOND EDITION:

Better to be the Disrupter than the Disrupted

"Don't wait for a couple of guys in a garage to come up with an idea that will upend your business."
—Linda Tischler, *Fast Company*[1]

Throughout the 1990s, Blockbuster mowed down its competitors in the video rental business by stocking a nearly unlimited number of copies of the latest Hollywood releases and using sophisticated inventory management systems that small rental stores couldn't match. Then in 2000—in what has since gone down in the history of corporate America as one of the biggest missed opportunities of all time—three guys pitched Blockbuster a crazy DVD-by-mail idea that eliminated late fees. They wanted $50 million, but Blockbuster literally laughed them out of the boardroom. "We're the industry leader," was the attitude, "Why would we need a niche business like yours. And do you know that we make half a billion dollars a year on late fees?"

Unfortunately, the very assets that Blockbuster thought were advantages turned out to be disadvantages and prevented them from seeing the future. Blockbuster's investment in traditional stores made it slow to recognize the value in online rentals and streaming video. (It's hard to change your thinking when you have 9,100 brick-and-mortar reasons not to.) Ten years later, Netflix was valued at $13 billion, and Blockbuster filed for bankruptcy.

Today, almost every organization in almost every sector resembles Blockbuster in some way. The scale and scope of changes that large established businesses face happens at unheard of speed, and the vast majority of them could benefit from a complete reinvention of their business. Generally, change presents itself as a crisis—a sudden change of circumstances beyond the company's control.

A crisis reveals a gap between what an organization is doing in the present and what it actually needs to do in the future. All of a sudden, you realize that you need to think about your business very differently. You recognize that the way you've thought about the business might have been a good fit for past circumstances, but now that those circumstances have changed, the old way of thinking is now a liability. The crisis provides a wake-up call—a bolt of energy that inspires disruptive leadership and action.

In its 17-year history, Netflix has had to reinvent itself three times: It started as a pay-per-rental DVD business and disrupted itself to become a subscription rental service. Then, new competitive threats forced it to go into streaming. (The company's market value dropped by 25% during the 3 months it took to make the transition.) When content providers saw how popular streaming had become, they raised their prices, which made it increasingly hard for Netflix to get content as thousands of movies and licensing deals expired.[2]

So Netflix started creating its own original content, such as *House of Cards* and movies like the sequel to Ang Lee's martial-arts epic *Crouching Tiger, Hidden Dragon*. Now, Amazon.com and other streaming competitors, along with more traditional networks such as HBO (which produces *Game of Thrones*) and AMC (*The Walking Dead*) are also creating original programming. If it's going to remain successful, Netflix will have to keep changing its thinking because no one actually knows how, or with what strategies, new or existing players will compete in the future.

In some cases, threats to a company's business model come less from direct competitors than from high-impact innovation in a seemingly unrelated market. Consider the transformative power of the fastest-selling devices in history: More than two billion people around the world use Internet-enabled smartphones. And they are, as the late Steve Jobs, then Apple's chief executive, prophetically proclaimed about the iPhone, changing everything.

For example, although we wouldn't truly consider smartphones and the telecommunications industry a direct competitor of the NYC Taxi and Limousine Commission, they have a huge impact on that market. Uber, now a household name operating in 55 countries around the world, uses a smartphone app and sophisticated data analysis to connect available drivers to nearby fares within minutes. You can use its apps to find a driver near you and ask to be picked up—it's essentially a remote control for taxis. Uber's business model could not have existed in a pre-iPhone world. (Mostly because of the iPhone, Apple is now worth more than any other company in the world.) But in fewer than five years, Uber has raised more than one-quarter of a billion dollars in venture-capital funding.

In my experience, working with everything from startups to Fortune 100 companies, it's difficult to recognize the need for disruptive thinking in non-crisis situations. The company concentrates on what it knows how to do best—and it views ideas for trying something to be distractions from the central task of running the core business.

The Italian eyewear conglomerate Luxottica had dominated the $65-billion-per-year industry since 1961, until four college friends started asking why they had to pay more for their glasses than for their smartphones? By designing and manufacturing their own frames and selling directly to consumers online, Neil Blumenthal, Andrew Hunt, David Gilboa, and Jeffrey Raider discovered they could charge as little as $95 per frame, a fraction of what a similar nice pair of glasses would cost at a Luxottica-supplied optical shop. Four years later, their company Warby Parker distributed its millionth pair of glasses, and Luxottica is operating with a renewed sense of energy, acquiring Glasses.com (which mimics Warby Parker's website) and launching a Warby-esque rebranding of the retail chain Pearle Vision.[3]

Disruptive change is essential, and sometimes the only way to save what was once the "right model at the time" is to destroy (or at least rethink) it. Nothing is too sacred to be reconsidered. No one way of doing things is beyond improvement. (How long did we put our luggage on top of a cart with wheels before it took someone to think of putting wheels directly under our suitcase?)

Yes, new ideas involve effort, complication, and risk—there's always something easier, simpler, and more certain to pay off than innovation. Yet every organization has squandered ideas—not through ignorance of their value, but because it was easier to avoid committing to a new way of operating. In the same sense, every organization underestimates the potential for finding new opportunities—we constantly fail to appreciate the many undiscovered opportunities that are out there.

The greater the uncertainty, the more ideas a business needs. And the more ideas you have, the surer you must be of the questions you're asking—or not asking.

Organizations must constantly ask themselves disruptive questions and then decide whether to reorganize around their answers.

Disrupt is about doing the work of crisis without the crisis.[4]

Disruptive Thinking:

The Revolution Is in Full Swing

"We do not merely want to be the best of the best.
We want to be the only ones who do what we do."
—Jerry Garcia, The Grateful Dead[1]

The old mantra, "differentiate or die," is no longer relevant. In fact, I'd argue that, today, there's actually too
much differentiation going on. By steadfastly clinging
to the "differentiate or die" mantra, businesses large
and small have made it extremely difficult for their
customers (and prospective customers) to tell the difference between deep, meaningful change and shal-
low, superficial novelty. As a result, with an excess of
similar offerings in the marketplace all claiming to be
"different" (which, theoretically, was supposed to add
value to a company's products or services), it's nearly
impossible for businesses to get their products noticed
and command a premium for their efforts.

Now, don't get me wrong; I'm not against differentiation as a business strategy. In fact, as creative director of a global innovation firm, frog design, I spent
a great deal of my time helping clients differentiate
their offerings in the marketplace. Unfortunately,
people are usually most comfortable with what's most
familiar—and the product, service, or business model

that they've experienced most often is the one that seems intuitively right. They become trapped by their existing perceptions, unable to recognize things they haven't seen before. As a result, I've watched too many clients spend huge amounts of money and resources trying to gain an edge on the competition by making *incremental* changes to their existing products and services.

This pattern of behavior is particularly common in successful companies operating in mature industries. They embrace incremental change because it supports their current business model. Reluctant to spend a bunch of money modifying their existing operations so they can make new things that will compete with their old things, these companies become complacent and stop innovating. Big mistake. Because when a business makes only incremental changes, they find themselves on a path that gets narrower and narrower. Eventually, they reach the end of the path, and by then, their customers have forsaken them for a new offering that nobody saw coming. In cases where companies do take disruptive risks, it's often because they're backed into a corner and there's no other choice.

Here's the bottom line: Companies that try to differentiate themselves by focusing on incremental innovation instead of game-changing, *disruptive* innovation will differentiate themselves right out of business. Companies simply cannot afford to wait until they get backed into a corner. They need to be consistently making bold moves, even at the very peak of their success. So, instead of "differentiate or die," the real mantra should be "differentiate all you want, but figure out a way to be the only one who does what you do, or die." Okay, that's a little cumbersome, but you get the point.

Thinking the Unthinkable

Figuring out a way to be the only one who does what you do is a provocative goal, but it's absolutely unobtainable unless you make some significant changes to the way you think about competition and the business you're in. I'm not talking about little tweaks here and there. I'm talking about a way of thinking that surprises the market again and again with exciting, unexpected solutions. A way of thinking that produces an unconventional strategy that leaves competitors scrambling to catch up. A way of thinking that turns consumer expectations upside down and takes an industry into its next generation. It's what I call *disruptive thinking*.

In the literature of innovation theory, the phrase "disruptive" is associated, in part, with the notion of "disruptive technology," which Clayton Christensen outlined in his book *The Innovator's Dilemma*. Christensen observes that disruptive technologies often enter at the bottom of the market, where established companies ignore them. They then grow in influence to the point where they surpass the old systems.[2] But, in our process—the one you'll be following in this book—disruptive thinking is not so much about how to spot and react to disruptive changes in technology and the marketplace; it's about how to *be* the disruptive change.

Being the disruptive change in an industry is exactly the sort of thing that new start-ups and small-scale enterprises are best at. But, as you'll soon see, it's a way of thinking that can be learned and applied just as effectively by large organizations and industry incumbents—in fact, by anyone who's willing to challenge the status quo wherever they are.

There is no better time to challenge the status quo than right now. Winning organizations in the next decade will be those that produce and implement ideas that are not easily conceived of or replicated by a competitor. Companies will create new categories and redefine old ones. Customers will fundamentally change what they want from the products and services they experience. The Internet and the infrastructure of massive connection have already reinvented many industries, but we've barely scratched the surface. We're still surrounded by countless products, services, and business models that are built on the logic of the past. (Just think of the current challenges for magazines, newspapers, and books.) Many of the decisions that define these businesses were made years ago, in a different age, and a different context.

Globalization, accessibility to an overwhelming array of products and information, and technological innovation are already rapidly changing the marketplace in significant ways. As a result, consumers are changing the way they buy, and businesses need to change the way they compete. We need to rethink the habits that have made us successful in the past, and challenge the conventional wisdom and industry models that have defined our world. In the words of marketing expert Seth Godin, "Industries are being built every day (and old ones are fading). The revolution is in full swing, and an entire generation is eager to change everything because of it. Hint: It won't look like the last one with a few bells and whistles added."[3]

To thrive in this new era, organizations and institutions, executives and entrepreneurs need to learn to think and act disruptively. To put it a little differently: Think what no one else is thinking, and do what no one else is doing.

Think what no one else is thinking, and do what no one else is doing.

Disruptive by Design

So, how do you go about making disruptive thinking part of your skill set? Well, it's not about hiring the right people or spending more money on training or traditional approaches to innovation. The good news is that schools around the world are already teaching disruptive thinking to their students. The bad news is that, instead of being taught in MBA programs, this new thinking style is taught in design schools.

Designers are taught to take conventions and turn them on their head—to make the ordinary unexpected. They create an emotional connection between a product or service and the prospective consumer. As best-selling author and critical thinker Dan Pink puts it, "Mastery of design, empathy, play, and other seemingly 'soft' aptitudes is now the main way for individuals and firms to stand out in a crowded marketplace."[4] Now, I'm not saying that MBAs don't have a place in the world or that designers have the answers to all life's questions (or at least the ones about business). Not at all. The problem is that design and business logic exist in parallel universes and rarely come in contact with one another. As a result, both disciplines suffer. Business schools teach how to analyze but not how to create compelling emotional connections, while design schools teach how to come up with those connections but not how to ensure they're commercially viable.

Either one by itself is nice, but to survive—and thrive—in today's business climate, you've got to have both. We urgently need to close the discipline gap and strip away the elite complexity (and yes, there's plenty of snobbism and elitism on both sides). We need to find a way to fuse the analytical rigor that has been the centerpiece of business competition for the last decade with the fluid, intuitive process of design. This is precisely the sort of juxtaposition disruptive thinking thrives on.

Savvy executives, managers, entrepreneurs, and venture capitalists are beginning to recognize that the game of transformation relies on this fusion. But, despite the fact that they recognize that design effort is important, most execs don't pay enough attention to it. For many, design effort is out of sight, out of mind, which is why people rarely use disruptive thinking skills outside the world of design.

Like it or not—and whether you can see it or not—design is everywhere. Every product, service, or business model, no matter how large or small, is designed. You might think of design as a skeleton. The bones that support our bodies aren't visible, but they're there. And just as our bones give shape to our bodies, design shapes our experience with every product, service, or business model we interact with.

The Goal of This Book

Paul Romer, an influential economist at NYU's Stern School of Business, defines *ideas* as "the recipes we use to rearrange things to create more value and wealth."[5] And the goal for any organization—no matter what the size—should be to generate a steady stream of new recipes—ideas that alter the trajectory of a business and revive stagnant markets or completely reinvent the competitive dynamics of an industry. And that's exactly what I teach you how to do in this book. Think of *Disrupt* as the business equivalent of a cookbook that provides you with the framework and motivation you need to discover and execute bold new recipes.

Over the course of this book's seven chapters, you'll learn to think about what usually gets ignored, pay attention to what's not obvious, and create disruptive solutions in a matter of days or weeks, not months or years. And by the time you're done, you'll find yourself asking, "Why hadn't we ever thought about our business and industry this way before?"

Five Stages of Disruptive Thinking

Disruptive thinking develops through a five-stage process:

1. Craft a disruptive hypothesis.

2. Define a disruptive market opportunity.

3. Generate several disruptive ideas.

4. Shape them into a single, disruptive solution.

5. Make a disruptive pitch that will persuade internal or external stakeholders to invest or adopt what you've created.

The book is organized into three parts. By the end of Part I, you'll have come up with three disruptive ideas—ideas that have potential but still need to be tested and refined. If you want to take those ideas to the next level, Part II will get you there by walking you through the process of gaining consumer feedback, transforming your ideas into solutions, and then pitching the results. Part III delves into the management of innovation and the disruptive leader's role in helping people (including themselves) out of their conceptual habits and biases. It explains the need to foster disruptive thinking and ensure that all employees know when and how to do it.

This is not a book you can pick up and start on page 50, read a few pages, and put down. Again, it's like a cookbook. For the best results, you need to follow the steps in order, just the way they're laid out. Here's a bit more detail on what each chapter covers.

Part I: The Hypotheses, the Opportunity, and the Ideas

Chapter 1—Crafting a Disruptive Hypothesis: Be Wrong at the Start to Be Right at the End

It all starts with a wild question. In simple terms, a hypothesis is the fill-in-the-blank part of the question, "I wonder what would happen if we _____ ." A lot of people would come up with minor tweaks, like a color change or a new feature or moving production overseas. But, that's not what we're looking for. If you don't shake things up with a few ideas from way, way out in left field, your brain will ensure that you'll process any new information and ideas using what you already know as a filter. And the result will be exactly the kind of thinking that maintains the status quo. The goal at this stage is to kick off the process with a disruptive hypothesis, a true game changer.

Chapter 2—Discovering a Disruptive Opportunity: Explore the Least Obvious

The next step is to take the hypothesis you just crafted and hone it to something usable. You'll start by looking at the real-world context your hypothesis will exist in. Who lives there now? What do they need? What motivates them? Defining a disruptive opportunity is designed to be quick and informal, intuitive and qualitative, and above all, accessible. It shouldn't take you more than two to three days, and, in many cases, you'll be able to do it in as little as two or three hours. The point I'm emphasizing is that *anyone* can (and should) feel empowered to go out and start creating new business ventures, products, and services without drowning in the sea of complexity that makes up typical market research projects.

Chapter 3—Generating a Disruptive Idea: Unexpected Ideas Have Fewer Competitors

Opportunities by themselves don't lead to profits or lasting change. So, the big question in this chapter is: How do you transform an opportunity into an idea? Well, the first thing to realize is that any old ideas won't do. We're looking for disruptive ideas—ideas that have the power to influence and to shape behavior. Ideas that stir the imagination and inspire a sense of possibility. Unfortunately, in my experience, most ideas never get anywhere near this level. We'll spend the last part of this chapter learning how to move past the stumbling blocks and generate the kind of disruptive ideas that transform a compelling opportunity into a commercial offering.

Part II: The Solution, and the Pitch

Chapter 4—Shaping a Disruptive Solution:
Novelty for Novelty's Sake Is a Resource Killer

Disruptive ideas are great, but they're only half the story. Unless you can make those ideas *feasible*, they can't deliver value. How do you know whether an idea is workable? Well, you don't, unless you actually see how it plays with your target market. Without testing your ideas with prospective end users and consumers, you're in danger of coming up with really terrific ideas that will completely flop when they hit store shelves. In this chapter, we change our focus from *conceiving* ideas to *transforming* them into practical solutions. Remember: There's a simple but critical difference between an idea and a solution: A solution is always feasible. If it's not, it's not really a solution.

Chapter 5—Making a Disruptive Pitch:
Under Prepare the Obvious, Over Prepare the Unusual

At this point, you've got a bit of a sales job on your hands. No, I'm not talking about selling to customers. Long before you get to that point, you'll need to sell your disruptive solution to the people within your organization or the external stakeholders who control the purse strings. So, be prepared: Most people don't embrace a disruptive solution because it's disruptive; they embrace it because they believe it will deliver value. And you're going to need a lot more than a basic presentation to earn that confidence. That's why the final output of this process is a 9-minute pitch that takes your audience from their initial, pre-presentation, "Why should I care about this?" through the mid-presentation, "I'm curious to see where this is going." attitude, to a post-presentation, "Hey, this is great! How do we implement it?"

Part III: The Disruptive Leader

Chapter 6—The Disruptive Leader's Motivation: A Different Attitude

What does it take to be a disruptive leader? Do you need to be a brilliant agitator like Steve Jobs? An obscenity-spewing trash-talker like T-Mobile's John Legere? A driven workaholic with a passion to change the world like Tesla's Elon Musk? Sure, CEOs like that get a lot of press, but there's more to success than being loud and charismatic. Truly disruptive leaders are like Master Chefs on a cooking show, always looking for ways to take existing ingredients—the same ones everyone else has access to—and combine them in unique ways. Those new recipes are a type of investment capital: the more you have, the better. Of course, not all of them will succeed. But disruptive thinking and leadership is less about the success of any one idea and more about putting your business in a position where you have more new ideas to spend than your competition does. Most importantly, being a disruptive leader is about creating a culture where everyone values new recipes. Because if you want to build a disruptive organization, you first have to build more disruptive leaders.

Chapter 7—The Disruptive Leader's Mindset: A Different Awareness

It's hard to imagine alternatives when you depend on a set of assumptions and habits, when that set of assumptions and habits serves you well, and when everyone around you has the same assumptions and habits. As the old saying goes, "It's difficult to get someone to understand something, when their salary depends upon them not understanding it." As a result of all this, an organization's range of actions is generally limited to what is comfortable and conventional. Disruptive leaders are able to steer clear of those traps. They constantly challenge their assumptions and habits and those of the people around them, and they expect to be challenged in return. Disruptive leaders have the power to see possibilities beyond what others have defined as limits, and the power to rethink what their organization is and what it might become. Most of all, they have the power to bring out those same powers in the people they lead.

How This Process Developed

While at frog design, I often noticed a huge disconnect between our approach to innovation and our clients' approach. Ours was fast, fluid, and intuitive. Theirs tended to be slow, rigid, and analytical.

What especially stood out was how paralyzing "innovation strategy" processes can be. A lot of the problem comes from requiring consensus on one step before moving on to the next one. The well-meaning intention is to ensure that the idea is aligned with strategy, allow the team to create buy-in, and give senior executives a variety of options.[6] Most of the time, this innovation process starts off pretty well, but inevitably, companies lose their momentum and their motivation. This is especially true in highly successful organizations. They get so bogged down in the complex details that they forget all about (or never had in the first place) "creative destruction," which is the need to fundamentally question their biggest achievements. As a result, instead of stimulating innovation, they end up stifling it.

So, you can imagine what happened when our clients decided they wanted to be part of the creative process. Listening to our proposals and making decisions wasn't enough. Oh, no. They wanted to contribute ideas and get involved in creating strategy and direction. Clearly, we needed to come up with a new approach for working together. If our clients were going to be involved in key parts of the process, the frog design teams would have to add a bit more structure to their free-flowing, intuitive approach. At the same time, the clients would have to get comfortable operating with a little *less* structure.

In the end, I developed a process that we called *frogTHINK*—a fast, agile approach to collaborative innovation that would maintain the right level of tension between fluid intuition and logical rigor. frog design has clients in virtually every business sector and of every size, from start ups to Fortune 100. With such a diverse group, we had to make the process accessible to everyone, regardless of educational and professional background. We also had to make it easy for clients to hit the ground running, to understand, participate in, and contribute to. No esoteric jargon or complex charts and equations. Also, no brainstorming with water pistols, beanbags, and other supposedly creativity-stimulating methods.

In 2005, I had the opportunity to take this process further by developing a new, graduate-level course at the Stern School of Business at NYU. The goal was to teach B school students how to solve problems and create opportunities using a disruptive thinking approach. The object wasn't to turn them into designers. (It was unlikely that any of them would continue on to be professional designers after business school anyway.) Instead, we tried to transcend design technique and focus on a business-design mentality.

The course is intended for people who have no previous background or training in—or even exposure to—design. We focus on helping students develop ways of thinking that are very different from those they would learn in a typical MBA environment. And, by the end of the course, they've learned the simple-yet-thorough process of disruptive thinking—the exact process we're going to spend the rest of this book discussing.

What This Book Is Not

This is *not* just another book on brainstorming. You've probably read plenty of them on idea generation, and you may even have participated in some brainstorming sessions, sitting around coming up with random ideas, hoping one sticks. Unfortunately, most idea-generation methods focus on quantity and not quality. They typically start out with the goal of solving a specific business problem, and then come up with as many ideas as they can that fit within the constraints of that problem. Worse yet, traditional brainstorming completely overlooks the issue of what to *do* with those ideas after they've been generated.

A step-by-step process

for imagining a powerful

market disruption

and transforming it

into reality.

My focus is to teach you tools that will force you out of your old thinking patterns. More importantly, we start off with the ideas and then bring in the business constraints later to shape them into something that has a high likelihood of succeeding in the market.

In short: This book is a step-by-step process for imagining a powerful market disruption and transforming it into reality—a disruptive approach for a disruptive age.

PART I

The Hypotheses, the Opportunity, and the Ideas

CHAPTER 1

Crafting a Disruptive Hypothesis:

Be Wrong at the Start to Be Right at the End

"I love tackling lazy industries."
—Richard Branson[1]

It all starts with a wild question: In Hollywood, it might be, "What would happen if a shark swam into a beach resort and attacked a swimmer?" *Jaws.* In architecture, someone must have wondered, "What would happen if we put the plumbing, electrical services, and air vents on the *outside* of a building instead of the inside?" *Pompidou Center, Paris.* In fashion, "What would happen if we sold socks in sets of three, where none of them match?" *Little Miss Matched.* In the video rental business, "What would happen if we didn't charge late fees?" *Netflix.*

Each of these innovations—which were revolutionary in their time—began with a *disruptive hypothesis*, a seemingly crazy way to fill in the blank part of the question, "I wonder what would happen if we...." It would have been easy to go for incremental tweaks, such as "...if we changed the color," or "...if we added a new feature," or "…if we moved our production overseas." But, disruptive hypotheses go way, way beyond that.

A disruptive hypothesis is an intentionally unreasonable statement that gets your thinking flowing in a different direction. It's kind of like the evolutionary biology theory of "punctuated equilibrium," which states that evolution proceeds slowly and every once in a while is interrupted by sudden change. Disruptive hypotheses are designed to upset your comfortable, business equilibrium and bring about an accelerated change in your own thinking.

Contrast this with the more traditional definition of "hypothesis," which is a best-guess explanation that's based on a set of facts and can be tested by further investigation. For example, you try to make a call on your cell phone and all you get is a blank screen. Based on that fact (the phone won't power up), you come up with a hypothesis: The battery may be dead, so if I charge the battery, the phone should work. You then test that hypothesis by charging the battery. If your hypothesis was correct, you should be able to make calls. If the phone is still dead, you'll need to formulate a new hypothesis and test it.

With a disruptive hypothesis, however, you don't make a reasonable prediction. (If I charge the battery, the phone will work.) Instead, you make an unreasonable provocation. (What if a cell phone didn't need a battery at all?) The difference between prediction and provocation, to paraphrase George Bernard Shaw's famous line, is the difference between "seeing things as they are and asking, 'Why?,' or dreaming things as they never were and asking, 'What if?'" [2]

In our fast-changing world, when business certainties are no longer certain, the ability to imagine things as they never were and ask, "What if?," is an essential part of every executive's skill set. So, the goal in this chapter is to start generating hypotheses that will enable you to radically reinterpret topics that everyone else in your industry has probably taken for granted.

"What would happen if we put the plumbing, electrical services, and air vents on the outside of a building instead of the inside?" Pompidou Center, Paris.

The ability to imagine things as they never were and ask, "What if?," is essential.

Harvard Professor Niall Ferguson has a genius for this form of provocation. Named by *Time* magazine as one of the planet's 100 Most Influential People, his radical theories force readers to refine their own thinking. "It's not about being a contrarian for its own sake," says Ferguson, "it's about being willing to test all hypotheses." [3] On the abolishment of slavery in Britain, for example, "It used to be argued that slavery was abolished simply because it had ceased to be profitable, but all the evidence points the other way; in fact, it was abolished despite the fact that it was still profitable. What we need to understand, then, is a collective change of heart."[4] Ferguson also takes a swipe at the conventional wisdom surrounding aspects of World War I. "The key to the Allies' victory was not an improvement in their ability to kill the enemy," Ferguson argues, "but rather a sudden increase in the willingness of German soldiers to surrender." [5]

As we go through the process of doing a little disrupting of our own, I want you to keep in mind the three following questions:

1. What do you want to disrupt?

2. What are the clichés?

3. What are your disruptive hypotheses?

What Do You Want to Disrupt?

As mentioned in the Introduction, one of the major hurdles facing today's executives and business leaders is how to meaningfully differentiate themselves from everyone else who's operating in the same space. To do that requires that you define the situation in the industry, segment, or category that you want to challenge. And by "situation," I mean the broad view from 10,000 feet. Here's what this might look like:

- This is an area in which everyone seems to be stuck in the same predicament and nothing has changed in a very long time.

- This is an area where profit performance is average—it really should be more successful than it is.

- This is a category where growth is slow and everything seems the same.

Once you have a situation to focus on, describe it in one sentence: "How can we disrupt the competitive landscape of *[insert your situation]* by delivering an unexpected solution?"

Whether you choose to think about an industry, segment, or category is up to you and your business needs. For example, if you owned a boutique hotel in San Francisco, you might describe your situation in one or more of the following ways:

- How can we disrupt the competitive landscape of the *Travel & Leisure industry* by delivering an unexpected solution?

- How can we disrupt the competitive landscape of the *Hotel segment* by delivering an unexpected solution?

- How can we disrupt the competitive landscape of the *Luxury Hotel category* by delivering an unexpected solution?

That's it. The important thing is that the high-level situation you choose is just that—high-level. It's essential that you resist the natural urge to start thinking in terms of specific "problems." I know this runs counter to conventional innovation- and business-planning approaches, where people are conditioned to think only in terms of finding solutions. But, let's put it this way: If you define your situation as, "How can we increase the price of our hotel rooms?," you've effectively confined your range of possibilities to only issues having to do with raising your room rates. It's possible that you could end up with a completely new solution to a very specific problem, but at this stage, such a narrow focus will greatly limit your options later.

What Are the Clichés?

Now that you've defined your situation, the next step is to identify the assumptions that seem to influence the way insiders (and often outsiders) think about an industry, segment, or category. In other words, what are the clichés—the widespread, hackneyed beliefs that govern the way people think about and do business in a particular space. If you pay attention, you'll notice that clichés are everywhere. (You'll also notice that, almost by definition, they've lost their ingenuity and impact.) In their book *Funky Business*, authors Jonas Ridderstrale and Kjell Nordström refer to the proliferation of business clichés as the surplus society: "A surplus of similar companies, employing similar people, with similar educational backgrounds, coming up with similar ideas, producing similar things, with similar prices and similar quality."[6]

Director Quentin Tarantino cites the film *Patriot Games* as a typical Hollywood action/drama that uses the conventional "the-hero-is-not-a-murderer" cliché: The reluctant hero, Jack Ryan (played by Harrison Ford) has "every reason to gouge out the eyes and cut off the head of the man who terrorized and tried to kill him, his wife, his children," says Tarantino. But how does the villain die? "He falls off the boat and hits his head on the motor. So it's accidental that the villain gets killed. The important thing is that the hero is not a murderer." Tarantino denies this cliché. In his movies, the hero is often a murderer (Uma Thurman's character in *Kill Bill*, for example). "I want people to take revenge when revenge comes."[7]

Consider the multi-billion dollar video gaming industry. Video consoles, which are a big chunk of that market, were dominated by two giants: Sony with its Playstation and Microsoft with its Xbox. Both were driven by several clichés. First, that the world is split into "gamers" and "nongamers." Second, that gamers mostly care about faster chips and more realistic graphics. Third, game consoles are expensive. And fourth, that people play video games sitting down, barely moving anything but their fingers.

Then, along comes Nintendo, a distant third player, which turned the gaming industry's clichés on their head. Nintendo's Wii is relatively cheap, has no hard drive, no DVD, has weak connectivity, and comparatively low processor speed. But, within weeks of its launch, Wii became a hit with consumers, thanks to its innovative motion controller, which integrates players' movements directly into the game.

With the Wii, you can play tennis, baseball, golf, and even bowling. You can sword fight and box, too. Nintendo opened up the console world to a huge demographic of people who never considered themselves gamers. As journalist Joshua Cooper Ramo observes, the Wii, "demolished the wall between real and virtual, eroded the idea that world was split into 'gamers' and 'nongamers,' and forced the competition to completely rethink the whole idea of a game... Wii killed the idea that a video game was something you played without breaking a sweat."[8]

With the Wii, Nintendo turned the gaming industry's clichés on their head.

Searching for Clichés

Just being told, "Okay, get out there and find those clichés," can be extremely daunting. So, here are a few tips that will help you jump-start the process.

Start by getting online and identifying a handful of direct competitors in the industry, segment, or category you're focused on. If there are dozens or hundreds of competitors, you can't possibly consider all of them. Instead, group together those with similar characteristics (such as size and resources), strengths (such as brand name, distribution), and strategies (such as high quality). [9] Select one or two competitors in each group that are pretty representative of the group as a whole. A total of three to six competitors are the ideal number to work with.

Now, do a little research on each competitor and make a list of the clichés that keep everyone doing the same thing, competing the same way, or operating with the same set of assumptions. The quickest and most efficient way to do this is to explore company websites, examine their advertising, and read what people are saying about the companies and their products on blogs and other social media platforms (such as Twitter, Facebook, and Amazon). It shouldn't take you more than two to three hours to get a good feel for the competitive landscape. If you have more time, make your research efforts as experiential as possible—order one of a company's products online or sign up for their service. If they have a brick-and-mortar presence, sample those products or services in person.

Keep your research activities quick and informal, intuitive and qualitative. And list any clichés you think are relevant. But to keep you from drowning in a sea of information, consider using the following three filters:

- **Product clichés:** What are the cliché features and benefits? What are the cliché product attributes that are advertised (convenience and reliability, for example)? Where are the cliché areas where the product competes (typical customers, typical geographies, and typical market size)? In the soft-drink industry, for example, some of the product clichés are as follows: Soda is inexpensive, it tastes sweet, and it's advertised as aspirational. (For example, if you want to be like [fill in the name of your favorite celebrity spokesperson], you have to drink Mountain Dew.)

- **Interaction clichés:** What are the cliché steps a customer experiences when buying and consuming their products and services? Is the interaction face-to-face? How frequently do customers purchase or use? In the rental car business, for instance, the prevailing interaction clichés include the following: face-to-face interaction with a service agent, completing a lot of paperwork, and renting vehicles by the day.

- **Pricing clichés:** What are the typical ways companies price their products and services and charge customers? Are they packaging products and services together or pricing them individually? Are they charging the customer directly or through a retail partner? Are they offering discounts or other incentives? In the magazine industry, the dominant pricing paradigm is a subscription-sale model, whereby the magazines offer a hefty discount (often more than 50 percent off the cover price) for annual subscriptions.

If you're searching for clichés with a team—or even if you're doing it alone—all you need to come up with is three or four for each of the filters just listed. This will give you a list of 9 to 12 clichés to work with as you develop your hypotheses. You're not trying to be comprehensive or get everyone to agree on what the clichés are. The point is to get those tired truisms on the table so you can confront them later.

Often, the more established and obvious the cliché, the greater the impact when it's challenged. If we eat at a restaurant, for example, we expect to select what we eat from a menu we review when we arrive. If we buy socks, we expect they'll be sold in pairs that match. We don't consciously think about these things because "that's the way it has always been." This is the paradox of identifying clichés—the most obvious and seemingly natural assumptions are the easiest to ignore. But, recognized or not, they still exert a powerful influence.

What Are Your Disruptive Hypotheses?

Now that you have a list of the clichés that are influencing the business situation you're focused on, your next goal is to start provoking the status quo. To do that, you'll take those clichés and twist them like a Rubik's cube and look at them from the inside out, upside down, backward, and forward. You're trying to find a way to rearrange the pieces, which in turn will provoke a different way of looking at the situation. Specifically, you're looking for something (or things) that you could scale up or scale down, move in the opposite direction, or completely do without.[10] Let's take a closer look.

Take the clichés and twist them like a Rubik's cube.

What Can You Invert?

In order for you to start moving in a new direction, you need to kick hard against what's already there. There are usually a number of different ways to inverse a given situation. If there's an action, look at the opposite action. If something is happening over time, run the time scale backward. If there's a one-way relationship between two parties, try changing the direction 180 degrees. As we saw with the soft-drink industry, some of the clichés are

- Soda is inexpensive.

- It tastes good.

- It's advertised as aspirational.

To start moving in a new direction, you need to kick hard against what's already there.

Inverting "soda is inexpensive," gives you "soda is expensive," and reversing "tastes good" gives you "tastes terrible," both of which sound completely ridiculous. But, you can't break the clichés without going through this step, which is exactly what Red Bull did. It placed absolutely no importance on taste;

the product is double the price of Coca-Cola. And Red Bull dispensed with marketing aspirational images. The message was that Red Bull may not necessarily make you feel happy, but it'll definitely give you a shot of energy when you need it.

Designer Tibor Kalman famously produced a series of deliberate cliché inversions designed to draw attention to multiculturalism and global awareness for *Colors* magazine. The Spring 1993 issue created an international stir on the topic of race by publishing full-page photos of the face of Queen Elizabeth II of Great Britain altered to look like a black woman, Pope John Paul II as an Asian, and filmmaker Spike Lee as a white man. That issue propelled *Colors* to international fame. "I'm always trying to turn things upside down and see if they look any better," [11] Kalman was fond of saying.

As both the Red Bull and *Colors* stories illustrate, inversions sometimes lead to significant breakthroughs.

What Can You Deny?
The denial method works by completely dumping key aspects of a cliché. Back to our rental car example for a minute, where the prevailing industry clichés include

- See the customer.

- Complete a lot of paperwork.

- Rent by the day.

What would happen if you no longer needed to see the customer, you got rid of the paperwork, and you started renting by the hour? Well, you'd end up with something very much like Zipcar, where there's no waiting in line, no papers to fill out, and no pressure to upgrade or add 27 different kinds of insurance. In fact, there's no face-to-face interaction at all. Customers apply to become members (or "zipsters") and they reserve vehicles online. The disruption?

- Don't see the customer.

- No paperwork.

- Rent by the hour.

With Zipcar, members pay an annual fee and then rent a car by the hour on a pay-as-you-go basis.

Many clichés are still around for no other reason than "we've always done it this way." Remember *The Cosby Show*? How about *Full House, Perfect Strangers,* and *Family Matters*? In the 1980s and early 1990s, the entire television sitcom lineup operated according to what the industry referred to as the "hugging and learning rule." Whatever tension developed during the first part of the show would be resolved at the end with all the main characters a little closer and a little wiser. Then, a show came along and started playing by a new rule: "no hugging, no learning." No matter how much trouble the characters got into, they never learned from their mistakes, and they never ended with a wholesome message. It was a breath of fresh air in a stale category, and it became one of the most successful sitcoms of all time: *Seinfeld.*

What Can You Scale?

Each of us has a well-trained and highly developed sense of the natural size and proportions of the world around us. So, when items in a given situation are out of proportion with each other, it comes as a shock and immediately grabs our attention. The advertising industry has successfully used this technique for decades to get us to pay attention to their ads.

But, when it comes to generating disruptive hypotheses, you're not exaggerating the scale simply to manipulate other peoples' attention. Instead, you're using the shock value to disrupt your *own* perception so you can look at the situation in a new way. What is scarce that could be made abundant? What is abundant that could be made scarce? What is expensive that could be free?

As I mentioned earlier, the pricing cliché in the magazine industry is a subscription-sale model, where publishers offer a significant discount for annual subscriptions. Typically, buying a subscription is 50 percent *less* than buying from a newsstand. Then, along comes a startup lifestyle magazine called *Monocle*, and instead of the traditional subscription-sale model, it created a subscription-*premium* model. The disruption? "Buying an annual subscription is *50* percent *more* than the cost of buying from a newsstand."

That high-priced subscription also gets you exclusive access to premium website content, signature products, social events, books, and audio programs. In its first year, the magazine's circulation was already 150,000, and it's currently sold in more than 50 countries.[12]

The Story of Little Miss Matched

There are all sorts of examples of companies that have been launched on the strength of their disruptive thinking. But one of my all-time favorites is Little Miss Matched. Jonah Staw, the co-founder and CEO of Little Miss Matched, used to work with me at frog design and is a poster boy for the kind of disruptive thinking that I espouse in this book. The company he co-founded with two other friends is a great example of how paying attention to the non-obvious and the seemingly mundane can lead directly to discovering areas where disruptive thinking can have an impact. At the end of each chapter, I'll briefly describe how the story of Little Miss Matched dovetails with the process you're reading about.

Think Outside the Socks!
The Disruptive Hypothesis

Jonah was having dinner with some friends in a trendy restaurant in San Francisco when the discussion turned to what he calls "disruptive business ventures." Suggestions were flying left and right, and at one point, someone asked, "How crazy would it be if some company started selling socks that didn't match?" Everyone thought it was a terrible idea— not particularly practical, certainly not useful, and difficult to own—and they moved on. Everyone, that is, except Jonah, who couldn't get the idea of mismatched socks out of his head. In his view, the sock category was lazy and boring; we're still buying and wearing socks the same way we have for decades. And, how many times have you lost one sock and had to toss the matching one—how much of a pain is that? It was a category of clichés ripe for disruption.

Then, on a vacation trip to Vietnam, Jonah made an important observation that convinced him that this disruptive hypothesis was worth experimenting with. He and his wife had visited a town that was known for clothing manufacturing. Just for fun, Jonah designed a jacket for his wife and got a beautifully made, finished product back in two days for about $15. Clearly, the apparel industry was far more accessible and had far lower barriers to entry than, say, consumer electronics, where it would cost hundreds of thousands of dollars to get a working sample of an idea. He returned to the U.S. eager to discover who would be interested in wearing mismatched socks.

We'll talk more about how this disruptive hypothesis eventually became a reality as we move through the rest of this book.

Taking Action

Your goal is to craft three disruptive "what if?" hypotheses for your situation: one inversion, one denial, and one exaggeration of scale.

Let's look at how this would apply to creating disruptive hypotheses for a new restaurant venture. As Nassim Nicholas Taleb, author of *The Black Swan: The Impact of the Highly Improbable*, explains:

> Think about the "secret recipe" to making a killing in the restaurant business. If it were known and obvious, then somebody next door would have already come up with the idea and it would have become generic. The next killing in the restaurant industry needs to be an idea that is not easily conceived of by the current population of restaurateurs. It has to be at some distance from expectations. The more unexpected the success of a venture, the smaller the number of competitors, and the more successful the entrepreneur who implements the idea.[13]

Here's how you kick-start the process of creating something "not easily conceived of by the current population of restaurateurs."

Invert

- **Cliché:** Restaurants provide customers with a menu when they arrive (interaction).

- **Hypothesis:** What if a restaurant provided customers with a menu only when they leave?

Deny

- **Cliché:** Customers pay for food and service (price).
- **Hypothesis:** What if customers were not charged for food and service?

Scale

- **Cliché:** Restaurants offer a three-course meal (product).
- **Hypothesis:** What if a restaurant offered a 30-course meal?

Remember, this exercise is designed to challenge your established way of looking at an industry, segment, or category.

The general rule is that the bolder your hypotheses, the fresher the perspective they offer. So, don't skip this step and don't worry if your "what if's" seem completely ridiculous. After all, at first glance, a restaurant that doesn't charge for food and service, offers a 30-course meal, and provides customers with a menu only when they leave, seems, well... absurd!

That is, until you eat at *El Bulli*—rated the best restaurant in the world a record four times (2002, 2006, 2007, and 2008). Founded by Ferran Adria—the chef considered to be the best in the world—no other restaurant does what *El Bulli* does. It is open only at night from April to September and is booked solid years in advance. Over 800,000 people call or email for a table each season.

At *El Bulli*, you're not merely paying for food and a three-course meal of dishes that you may have eaten somewhere else. But rather, it's a five-hour experience of 30 courses unlike anything you've tried before. The meal costs 250 euros (close to $320 U.S.), but what *El Bulli* is really charging for are the hours of creativity, testing, and refinement behind the development of new dishes. "We have turned eating into an experience that supersedes eating," says Ferran. [14] At the end of their meal, guests receive a menu from the kitchen detailing the 30 courses they consumed, signed by the chef—a memento of their personal *El Bulli* experience.

After going through all the exercises in this chapter, you should be able to generate three brilliant, wacky, disruptive hypotheses. These will help you imagine radically new scenarios, ask unconventional questions, and discover unexpected advantages as you proceed through the process. Now, while that's a huge accomplishment, hypotheses aren't really worth much all by themselves. In the next chapter, we start the process of taking those hypotheses and gaining the customer insight necessary to turn them into opportunities.

CHAPTER 2

Discovering a Disruptive Opportunity:

Explore the Least Obvious

> "The most important advances are the
> least predictable ones."
> —Sir Francis Bacon[1]

People often say, "Apple doesn't do consumer research." This usually precedes an argument against the need for market research of any kind. But, the designers at Apple do conduct research—it's just not the traditional kind you read about in consumer behavior textbooks. It's informal, impromptu, and driven by acute observations of the context in which their products are used. Being insightful isn't a question of talent; it's a question of awareness.

Awareness is essentially being mindful of the cultural and social constructs that surround you and the people for whom you are creating something new. You've felt it before. The moment you decide you're going to buy a yellow MINI Cooper, you start seeing them all over town. Of course, they were there before, but the difference is that now your awareness has been focused.

All the Apple designers I've met share this awareness of context, which may explain why they're often sensitive to critical details that their competitors overlook. They examine the context for themselves rather than having it described by someone else. Jonathan Ive describes his observations of people interacting with Mac computers in an Apple store: "When people are looking at Macs in stores, they're drawn to them in a very physical way. They don't mind moving them around or touching them."

That observation lead him to an important insight: "You're seldom intimidated by something that you can feel. If you're intimidated by an object, you tend not to want to touch it."[2]

So, for Apple, there was an opportunity to give people a tangible sense of control over the technology by establishing an immediate physical connection between the user and the computer.

Think again about the statement "people are seldom intimidated by something they want to touch." That's an insight that wouldn't have been possible without close, unobtrusive observation of people interacting with technology. To cultivate insights and uncover opportunities, you need to observe the telling moments that reveal what consumers actually feel and do (as opposed to what they say they feel).

In Chapter 1, you identified a number of clichés, got rid of some of them, inverted and exaggerated the scale of others—and you came up with three disruptive hypotheses. But, hypotheses don't exist in a vacuum. The people you expect to experience the shift you're describing must believe that the change delivers value. So, when you consider how to put your hypotheses into action, you must stay focused on who's involved in the situation and their needs.

Why is this important? Because disruption for disruption's sake is just annoying. The reason most hypotheses fail to make it past the "what if" stage isn't that they're too radical; it's that the advantages of the disruption aren't clear. Or, put a little differently, it's not their lack of creative differentiation; it's their lack of customer insight.

Being truly insightful—and I'll show you exactly how to do that—involves immersing yourself into the world of your customers to try to see how things look from their viewpoint. The focus is on watching, not on talking. We'll start by looking at the real-world context your hypotheses will exist in. Who lives there now? What do they need? What motivates them? It's all about taking those hypotheses and translating them into actionable opportunities.

Be Quick and Informal

Officially, the methods of understanding the context I'm describing in this chapter fall under the general heading of ethnographic or contextual research.[3] The name isn't important. This research, whatever you want to call it, is designed to be quick and informal, intuitive and qualitative, and above all, accessible. It shouldn't take you more than two or three days and, in many cases, it can be done in as little as two or three hours.

Of course, you could go out and spend several months and tens of thousands of dollars on detailed demographic and psychographic market segmentation, focus groups, and quantitative studies. But, I think you'll get much better information—particularly while you're at the beginning of creating something new—by simply watching what people do and asking a few well-planned questions. That's something you can usually do for free or close to it. The point I'm emphasizing is that anyone can (and should) feel empowered to go out and create new business ventures, products, and services, without drowning in the sea of complexity that makes up typical market research projects.

Just to clarify: I'm not claiming that this process is comprehensive. It's not supposed to be. It is, however, an effective way to start developing qualitative observations. You'll be able to go through the process quickly, and you'll know early on whether it's working. If it is, you move on to the next step. If not, you can go back, tweak it, and do it again without losing much time or money.

After you gather that information and determine your context, you'll organize, filter, and prioritize your observations and transform them into meaningful insights.

What Are Your Observations?

Before you dive too far into your research, you need to have a clear idea of the core questions that you want answered. These aren't questions that you're necessarily going to directly ask customers. (You may ask some of them, but you'll get a lot of the information you're looking for through observation.) Your research goals will be influenced by the provocative hypotheses you created in Chapter 1, and you'll want to focus on the relationship between the customer and the industry, segment, or category:

- How and where do customers interact with the current products and services in your industry, segment, or category?

- What steps do they have to take to purchase products and services?

- How does the industry, segment, or category make the customer feel?

- What is the social network of the customer?

- Is the customer loyal to an existing product, service, or brand?

- What is the level of customer support offered?

Of course, before you can start observing anyone, let alone asking questions, you must have a general idea of whom to watch and speak. You definitely want to connect with a group that business consultant Robert Gordman calls *must-have customers*—the customers who share similar characteristics and are currently the most profitable ones in the situation you're focused on. Target people based on demographics (such as gender, age, marital status, education, and so on) and some situation-specific characteristics (such as foodie, early adopter, technophobe, and so on). But, don't let yourself get too boxed in by those standard segmentations. At the same time, don't forget the outliers—the people no one in your industry is looking at. These folks could turn out to be the most important group of all.

For example, I was recently involved with a project to design a new TV remote control. Our research team at frog design did tons of in-home visits. We spent hours watching people in action, learning about what they liked and what they hated about their current remotes. We also sent a team out to meet with blind people to observe how they used remotes and talk to them about the features they preferred and how they liked the buttons to be clustered. Traditional market research would never have bothered with blind consumers. But, the insights we generated from those visits were invaluable. After all, how many times have you been watching TV in the dark and changed the channel instead of turning up the volume because you couldn't see the buttons?

After you've got a handle on your research goals, your next task is to figure out how to do the actual observing. I've summarized my three favorite methods:

- **Pre-arranged, open-ended interview and observation.** This is the most common type of study. As the name implies, while you're asking questions designed to get your interview subjects to speak freely, you're also carefully observing the environment they live or work in and what they're doing while they're there. This is exactly what Intuit's "Follow Me Home" program was designed to do when the company was creating Quicken, its money-management software product. Engineers spent hours in real customers' homes watching their behavior and identifying their real needs. Then, they went back to their cubicles and incorporated what they'd learned into the next version of the program.

  "When the Quicken team came to my house, I thought they just wanted to find out how they could better advertise to me and people like me, but it wasn't that at all," said Wendy Padmos, one of dozens of volunteer participants in the program. "It was much more customer-focused. They wanted to know how I used their product, what was important to me, and what was not important to me. I told them I would like the ability to see my current spending against my average spending over the last 12 months, and now it's in the product!"[4]

- **Noninvasive observation.** Because of constraints such as time or access, you may have to make your observations in public environments without prior permission. This can reveal a lot of information, especially in high-density areas. Because you're operating in common public space, there's no need to schedule your observations (and you shouldn't anyway).

  There's a great story about the architect Louis Kahn and how he designed the green spaces between the buildings of the Salk Institute. Supposedly, Kahn, in his original plan, didn't include any marked or paved pathways through the grassy areas. Instead, he observed pedestrian traffic and eventually created paths that corresponded exactly with the routes people were really taking. How many times have you seen beaten trails that veer off from marked or paved paths?

- **Intercept.** This approach includes visiting a store, watching the purchase process or general customer interactions, and approaching people to speak with. Your aim is to understand how people make purchase decisions (or decisions not to purchase) right while it's happening.

  The observation method(s) you opt for will depend on a number of factors, including your budget, time schedule, and the people you're planning to observe. For example, if your target group includes elderly diabetics, you'll probably want to spend at least some time doing in-home visits. Home visits might work for a teen population, too, but you'll also want to hang out at shopping malls and at midnight screenings of the latest vampire movie.

What, Exactly, Am I Looking For?

The most common question I hear when people are new to contextual research is, "What am I looking for?" The most common answer is "pain points." Unfortunately, in most cases, that's the wrong answer. Business people are trained to focus only on problems—things that don't work and need fixing. They live by the motto, "If it ain't broke, don't fix it."

The most highly rewarded managers are often those who can quickly identify critical problems, analyze complex sets of data, and apply razor-sharp reasoning to come up with a solution. Most managers have become experts at this process, and they're motivated (often by hefty performance bonuses) to reach an endpoint or conclusion as soon as possible. Ultimately, I think that most researchers are trying to identify problems to solve.

However, actually coming right out and saying so usually causes immediate paralysis. The researcher becomes so preoccupied with spotting the big "broken" problems that he or she completely ignores everything else. Problems are also seductive because they're usually clear. The customers' frustration is visible and, even as an outsider, it's easy to empathize. But, more often than not, it's the small, seemingly unbroken aspects of a situation that provide the richest opportunity areas for innovation. These are often the nagging issues that linger for a long time without receiving much attention. They tend to be the things we ignore, precisely because they don't change.

It's the seemingly unbroken aspects of a situation that provide the richest opportunities for innovation.

Consider the humble can of house paint. For years, cans of paint have been made of tin and opened the same way: pried open with a screwdriver. But then, Dutch Boy Paint came along and introduced the Twist & Pour, an all-plastic gallon container featuring an easy twist-off lid and a neat-pour spout, which reduces the spilling and dripping typically associated with traditional paint cans. A molded handle allows for a more controlled pour and easier carrying. Adam Chafe, Dutch Boy's director of Marketing says, "Consumers told us the Twist & Pour paint container was a packaging innovation long overdue."[5] As this example shows, a satisfactory way of doing something (like opening a can of paint with a screwdriver) may be far from optimal.

So, instead of large pain points, you should spend your time looking for—and addressing—something much more subtle: small "tension points," the things that aren't big enough to be considered problems. The challenge, however, is that tension points are usually hard to spot, because the symptoms are easy to overlook. They're not screaming for attention the way "real" problems are. They're typically little inconveniences that people have grown complacent about.

The Twist & Pour paint container by Dutch Boy was a packaging innovation long overdue.

Tension points are a lot easier to identify after you have an idea of what to look for. Here are four specific types:

- **Workarounds:** These quick, efficient-seeming solutions address only the most obvious symptoms of a problem, not the underlying problem itself. Workarounds can actually be dangerous because, when symptoms clear up, people lose any incentive they may have had to deal with the real issues. Over the long term, the problem gets worse and, eventually, someone will have to come up with another workaround. In systems thinking, this vicious cycle is referred to as "shifting the burden."

Author Seth Godin has his own term for workarounds, which he describes in a blog post: "Global warming a problem? Just shave the bears. Let's define 'bear shaving' as the efforts we make to deal with the symptoms of a problem instead of addressing the cause of the problem. A rare Japanese PSA (public service announcement) showed a girl shaving a bear so it could deal with global warming."[6]

In a frog design project for one of the big three automakers, we learned that, in the words of project lead, Mike LaVigne, "There's much more happening than just going for a drive." Mike and his team discovered that a lot of people check email, make phone calls, and use their laptop while they're in their cars, even though the in-car experience wasn't designed to support those activities.

Keep your eye out for quick and ready fixes that people have created to "work around" less than ideal situations (Post-It notes on a computer screen, for example).

- **Values:** People's values play an important role in their motivations. What do they value? What's important to them? What's not? Men and women, for example, shop in different ways. Numerous studies have shown that women are especially interested in establishing a rapport and relationship with a knowledgeable salesperson. Men are more motivated by the proximity of parking to the front door of a place they're considering shopping in. Tension is often present when a product, service, or experience is in conflict with the values they find desirable. This can reveal important shifts in the qualities consumers find meaningful.

In his article for *Wired* magazine, "The Good-Enough Revolution," Robert Capps outlines a change in consumer values that he calls the MP3 effect:

> What has happened with the MP3 format and other Good-Enough technologies is that the qualities we value have simply changed. And that change is so profound that the old measures have almost lost their meaning…. We now favor flexibility over high fidelity, convenience over features, quick and dirty over slow and polished. Having it here and now is more important than having it perfect. These changes run so deep and wide, they're actually altering what we mean when we describe a product as "high-quality." [7]

Capps lists Netbook computers, e-book readers, Skype video conferencing, a Kaiser Permanente "microclinic,"and even the MQ-1 Predator plane as examples of the MP3 effect.

Look for high-priority and low-priority values. Has there been a change in what consumers' value in the products and services they buy? Has that change revealed a gap between what consumers want and what's actually available?

- **Inertia:** Generally, the more established people's habits, the higher the inertia, meaning they're less motivated to consider alternative choices. Many banking customers, for example, say that they dislike their bank and would be delighted to switch. But, the prospect of closing all of their accounts and reopening them somewhere else is so overwhelming that it's easier to just stay where they are. The same kind of thing happens in many other sectors, such as telephone or television services. Wherever customers feel trapped by inertia in a situation they find less than desirable is where you'll find tension. Keep an eye out for situations in which customers act out of habit. Opportunities can be created to either break or leverage that inertia.

In October 2005, Bank of America identified an opportunity to encourage consumers to open new accounts. The bank discovered a key point of inertia—people often round the amount of their financial transactions up to the next dollar because it's faster and more convenient. Could that inertia be leveraged to turn a habit of losing money into a habit of saving money? The result is a program called Keep the Change, in which, each time you make a purchase with a Bank of America Visa debit card, the bank rounds up the amount to the nearest dollar and transfers the difference into your savings account. Since its launch, over 700,000 have opened new checking accounts, and 1 million have set up new savings accounts.[8]

- **Shoulds versus wants:** People often struggle with the tension between *wants*, which are things they crave in the moment, and *shoulds*, which are the things they know are good for them in the long term. In their column for *Fast Company* magazine, Dan and Chip Heath make the case that "People need help saving themselves from themselves, and that presents a business opportunity."[9] They reference the work of Katherine Milkman, a doctoral student at Harvard Business School. Milkman has studied the way customers wrestle with wants and shoulds, and she suggests bundling the two. For example, the Heath's write, "exercising is a should, so what if your gym offered to receive your magazine subscriptions? That way, if you wanted to read the new *Vanity Fair* (a want), you'd have to drop by the gym. Or, what if Blockbuster offered you a free tub of popcorn (a want) for every documentary (a should) that you rented?"[10]

Look for the tension that lies between wants and shoulds. Treat all customers as highly invested in moving from where they are to where they want to be. Do they need help "saving themselves from themselves" to get there?

A Few Final Tips

Ideally, you should do your research in teams of two or three, instead of by yourself. Have one person do the interviews and one (or more) observe and record participants' behavior.

Remember that the customer is the expert and plays the lead role in the conversation, while you listen and probe with follow-up questions. That kind of dialog enables you to clarify details and avoid misunderstandings about what people do and why.

Stay focused on observing. Sure, you'll ask some questions, but unfortunately, that's not always the best way to gather information. In fact, it can often be misleading. People comment only on what they know and have experienced. They may well point out problems and defects, but they're much less able to suggest new insights. Their obvious needs are not the only ones and the non-obvious needs are often the richest source of new insights.

Make sure you document everything you're doing in at least two ways. This includes notes (handwritten or typed), photographs, video, audio, participant output in the form of drawing, writing, survey, digital entry, and so on. At the least, use notes and photographs.

Finally, don't edit yourself. You can always cut later.

Observations aren't any good when they're stuck in your head or stored on your laptop.

What Did You Find Out?

After you complete your field research and have your observations, the next step is to make sense of your discoveries. Observations aren't any good when they're stuck in your head or stored on your laptop. You need to make them tangible and get them out and onto a physical space. There's a variety of ways to do this, but they all involve putting your observations on paper. You can use regular paper, card stock, Post-It notes, or anything else that works for you. Aim for one observation per Post-It note or card. And don't forget to print out any photos you took. At frog design, we call this process "grounding the data."

The next step is to take all those pieces of paper, photos, and any other memory aids (notes you took on the back of a napkin, brochures, business cards, and so on) and transfer them to what we call an "insight board." At frog design, we use a large foam-core board, around 10–12 feet tall, 4–5 feet wide, which we lean against a wall. (You probably won't need anything that big—a white board, bulletin board, a large sheet of butcher paper, or even a kitchen table is just fine.) Insight boards allow you to see all of your research findings together.

I realize that what I'm describing here sounds (and actually is) hopelessly low-tech. Some digital tools enable you to do roughly the same thing, but our goal here is to get you to close your laptop. There's something about writing your ideas on paper and physically moving them around that makes the entire process feel more real to everyone involved. It also makes it easier to organize your thoughts, and it can help you stay out of some easy-to-fall-into thinking traps.

Set up an "Insight Board."

In their book *The Myth of the Paperless Office*, Social Scientists Abigail Sellen and Richard Harper agree that when it comes to performing certain kinds of creative tasks, paper has many advantages over computers:

> Because paper is a physical embodiment of information, actions performed in relation to paper are, to a large extent, made visible to one's colleagues.... Contrast this with watching someone across a desk looking at a document on a laptop. What are they looking at? Where in the document are they? Are they really reading their e-mail? Knowing these things is important because they help a group coordinate its discussions and reach a shared understanding of what is being discussed.[11]

With your observations in a tangible form, it's time to organize them into themes. So, where do you start?

When people get back from doing their contextual research, they normally have a few key takeaways bouncing around their heads, the big observations that they feel they've made, or the things that really excite them. These are the observations they talk about most, the first words out of their mouth when someone asks, "Hey, what did you find out?" Unfortunately, people's excitement about these key observations can blind them to everything else. They may consider other observations, but they'll eventually loop back around to the key ones. After those key observations have taken hold (which happens on a mostly subconscious level), it's almost impossible to shift your perspective, and your ability to recognize patterns is crippled.

Because those key observations are going to be on your mind, you might as well start working with them first. So, start searching through your other notes for observations that potentially have a connection to the key ones, and cluster them together. As you're going through this process, you'll undoubtedly find other observations that are connected in some way. Make clusters for those groups as well. After a while, you'll probably find that you can start grouping clusters together into larger themes. On the car project, for example, we identified the broad theme of "being prepared," which was made up of the following observations of how drivers used their vehicles:

- Collect things "just in case" (gloves, jumper cables, first-aid kit, camera)

- Keep things handy for an extra side trip (items for a hobby, bottle opener, blanket)

- Carry extra things to make a trip more comfortable (CDs, tissues, lip balm, water)

Organize your observations into themes.

Coding Your Observations

It's always a good idea to use different colors, paper sizes, or markings of some kind to code your key observations, supporting observations, and themes. I use different sized and shaped Post-It notes, but you can use anything you want, as long as it's consistent and everyone understands what means what. For example, you might start out with all of your observations on yellow notes. After you identify the key observations, write those on blue notes. After you cluster and organize, mark your themes with a green note.

The point of organizing observations into themes is to lay the foundation for generating insights.

Organize observations into themes so you can lay the foundation for generating insights.

What Are Your Insights?

There's a wonderful *New Yorker* article titled "The Eureka Hunt."[12] It's the story of a firefighter named Wag Dodge who survived an out-of-control fire in the Mann Gulch, Montana, in 1949. Thirteen other smoke jumpers died in the fire. But, Dodge was saved by a brilliant insight. Fleeing for his life, he suddenly stopped running and ignited the ground in front of him. He then lay down on the smoldering embers and inhaled the thin layer of oxygen clinging to the ground. The fire passed over him and, after several terrifying minutes, Dodge emerged from the ashes, virtually unscathed. What sort of a crazy person stops running from a fire and starts another one? Well, if you know certain things about fire and oxygen, knowledge that may have taken years to acquire, it's not as nutty as it sounds.

The Mann Gulch fire example is, admittedly, a bit extreme. And it probably has you wondering whether it's possible to learn how to produce insights or if you have to wait until a bolt of lightning hits you. To the latter, the answer is a definite *No.*

While some insights do spontaneously appear, most are generated through a process of organizing, filtering, and prioritizing all the great observations you've gathered and translating them into something meaningful—and actionable. In other words, insights are the product of synthesis. At first glance, an insight may seem like it came out of nowhere. But, when you think about it, you realize in hindsight that it makes perfect, logical sense. What happens is that you (sometimes unconsciously) recognize a pattern that enables you to see things in a new way—the kind of thing that makes you slap your forehead and say, "Why didn't I think of that before?" Albert Einstein put it succinctly when he said insight "comes suddenly and in a rather intuitive way. But intuition is nothing but the outcome of earlier intellectual experience." Even seemingly mundane observations can yield unexpected, yet logical insights. It's just a question of learning how.

It's important to recognize that observations and insights are not the same thing. Observations are raw data, the gradual accumulation of research information that you have consciously and carefully recorded—exactly the way you way you saw or heard it, with no interpretation. Insights are the sudden realizations—sometimes described as "Aha!" or "Eureka!" moments—that happen when you *interpret* the observations and discover unexpected patterns. Patterns reveal gaps between where people are and where they'd ideally like to be—between their current reality and their desires. Rifts between the way something is now and the way people assume it should be.

One classic example of a pattern revealing a gap is what's sometimes called "feature creep," the constant adding of more and more features to tech products that were already too complicated to begin with. Do you have a video camera? If so, how many of the features do you really use? How many do you really care about? All most people really want is to record, zoom, and upload the video to their hard drive or YouTube.

Consumer electronics company, *Pure Digital*, saw a way of greatly simplifying life (Pure Digital was acquired by Cisco Systems in 2009[13]). Home-video cameras were expensive and complicated, and it suspected there might be a place for a much cheaper, simpler video camera. So its team created the Flip Ultra to fill the gap, a video camera that has an On/Off switch, a zoom-in/zoom-out toggle, and a foldout USB adapter. And it runs on ordinary batteries.

The Flip Ultra video camera was created to fill a gap.

Wherever there's tension (observation), there's a gap. If you can spot the gap (insight), you can fill the void (opportunity).

Look for What's Unexpected and Ask, "Why?"

At this point, your insight board should have several observation clusters and themes. Because there's no way you can focus on the entire board at one time, what you're doing here is trying to find some good places to start.

Where you start is important, because it can make a big difference in the way you synthesize insights. We all have a tendency to focus on the most obvious information first—the information that confirms our existing knowledge. That's fine, but if you pay attention only to what's obvious, chances are that you're looking for corroboration and not wanting to reverse the opinions you already have. Insights don't come from looking at the obvious. They usually come from surprising sources, and, more often than not, they come from observations that were completely unexpected. These observations fly under the radar, unnoticed by people close to the situation. John Kounios, a psychologist at Drexel University, describes insight as "an act of cognitive deliberation transformed by accidental, serendipitous connections."[14]

Back in 1992, some residents of a small Welsh town called Merthyr Tydfil were participating in a clinical trial of a new angina drug. Unfortunately for the pharmaceutical company, the drug didn't do much for angina. But, the drug did have a lot of side effects in men, including back pain, stomach trouble, and erections. If everyone at Pfizer had stayed focused on finding an angina drug, it would have stopped the trials and dropped the drug. But, by shifting the focus from the obvious to the unexpected, from primary effects to side effects, it generated the insights that became one of the most successful drugs ever: *Viagra*.

When you identify something unexpected, spend some time looking for additional observations that may. suggest interrelated connections. Then, ask, "Why is this a pattern?" and, "Why is this unexpected?," and ultimately, "Why is this meaningful?" Asking "why?" encourages you to think through the connections between observations and adds a layer of interpretation.

Consider the mundane act of mopping a floor. On an assignment for Procter & Gamble, Boston-based consultancy, Continuum, went to work studying dirt, watching people clean, and cleaning floors themselves. As you'd expect, the obvious thing they observed was that people find mopping a disagreeable chore. However, they also made an unexpected observation—water doesn't remove dirt all that well. Asking "why?," they discovered a counterintuitive rift between expectation and result—between what people thought a mop was doing and what, in fact, it was doing. Instead of removing dirt, water tends to slop it around. Dry rags on the other hand, thanks to electrostatic attraction, are far more effective at picking dirt up. Customers didn't desire mops that work better with water. They just want clean floors.

This insight exposed a gap: an opportunity for waterless cleaning products. The Swiffer brand, as it became known, was an instant hit for P&G, with first-year sales of $200 million. P&G now earns more than $500 million annually from waterless cleaning products, and the insight remains unexpected. "How can it possibly work without water?" consumers often ask.[15]

The insight for waterless cleaning products was based on an unexpected observation—water doesn't remove dirt all that well.

Generating insights like this is really a pattern-recognition skill. In other words, you aren't just reporting what you observe as you observe it. Rather, based on everything you know and have experienced, you're making connections and interpreting the patterns you see. Insights are new configurations of knowledge that enable you, and others, to see the situation in a different, and often, counterintuitive way—one that draws attention to gaps that had been previously ignored.

Capturing Your Insights

Record your insights in real time and add them to your insight board (using a different colored Post-It note). Keep going until you have covered all of your key themes. Aim for a minimum of one insight per theme.

When capturing and describing insights, the words and phrasing you use matter. Insights often fly in the face of conventional wisdom or expectations. When that happens, use a well placed "but" or "whereas" to draw attention to the contradiction and increase the statement's impact. For example, here's how Continuum captured insights on some other projects: [16]

- Drivers of high-performance cars are not stressed by high-speed driving *but by parking.*

- Men who buy premium audio systems like to display them in their living rooms, *whereas women would rather hide them* behind plants or furniture.

- Customers are not interested in locks per se *but in the possessions those locks protect.*

Finally, be prepared to take risks with your insights. They don't have to be unmistakably correct; they have to be thought-provoking. In many research approaches, the pressure to be incontrovertibly right is so strong that there's no space for intuition and intriguing perspectives. The most important thing to remember is that research insights are not ends in themselves. You're generating them to feed the opportunities that will put your hypotheses into action.

To summarize: The first purpose of this research is to observe, identify, and record tension points. The second is to cultivate insights that highlight gaps between the way something is now and the way it ought to be. The third is to work out opportunities to fill the gaps.

What Are Your Disruptive Opportunities?

Now that you've captured a handful of insights, it's time to synthesize them into key areas of opportunity. To do that, you need to bring back your disruptive hypotheses—the three wacky and provocative "what if" questions I talked about in Chapter 1.

To recap: The reason you kick off this process with disruptive hypotheses instead of going straight into contextual research is because you must pick apart the existing industry clichés to see things differently. Provocative "what if" questions prepare you to recognize things you didn't notice before and put research observations together in new ways.

If you skip the hypothesis step, it probably wouldn't occur to you that there may be other ways of designing the situation you're focused on that are just as plausible (renting cars by the hour or socks that don't match, for example).

But, as I said at the start of this chapter, it's not enough to hypothesize about how something could be disruptive; your hypotheses have to be radical in ways that deliver value to people. And that happens only when you use customer insights to translate your hypotheses into opportunities.

Think of it this way: Hypotheses feed observations. Observations feed insights. *Insights feed opportunities.*

Moving from Insights to Opportunities

An opportunity has three distinct parts: There's an opportunity to provide [*who?*] with [*what advantage?*] that [*fills what gap?*]. In our car example, it might look like this:

"There's an opportunity to provide drivers with ways of being more productive that are safe and optimized for driving."

To get from insights to opportunities, start by matching each insight to the hypothesis it's most closely related to. Look for the insights that have the potential to put a hypothesis into effect—something in the insight that suggests that your implied disruption would deliver a key *advantage*. To continue the car example:

Hypothesis: What if cars were not for driving?

Insight: There's much more happening in a vehicle than just going for a drive, but cars are not designed to support non-driving activities.

After you find the best pairing, use the relevant insight(s) to work out one really big point of advantage for each of your "what if" speculations. (Renting cars by the hour would deliver *flexibility*. Miss-matching socks would enable *self-expression*.)

If you're in the soft-drink business, for example, and your disruptive hypothesis is that the product should taste terrible, is there an insight that indicates how you can turn that into an advantage? If your hypothesis suggests that your product should be far more expensive than the competitors', is there an insight that could make that into a good thing?

Back to the car example: The first part of the insight was "there's much more happening inside a vehicle than just going for a drive." This came from the observation that drivers currently check email, make phone calls, and use their laptop while in their cars.

If we imagine that cars were not for driving, and ask what else could they be used for, our insight suggests an advantage—people could use cars like an office to be more *productive*.

Hypothesis: What if cars were not for driving?

Insight: There's much more happening inside a vehicle than just going for a drive (checking email, making phone calls, using their laptop, and so on).

Opportunity: Provide drivers [who] with ways of being more productive [advantage].

The second thing to work out is "what's the *gap* that needs to be filled?" If this isn't immediately apparent, consider the tension point captured by the insight. If necessary, refer to the four categories I noted earlier:

- **Workarounds:** Does the insight suggest an opportunity to remedy the underlying problem itself, not just the symptoms?

- **Values:** Does the insight suggest an opportunity to address a change in what consumers' value?

- **Inertia:** Does the insight suggest an opportunity to leverage a habit or break a habit?

- **Shoulds versus wants:** Does the insight suggest an opportunity to turn wants into shoulds? Or shoulds into wants?

In the car example, the second part of the insight was "but cars are not designed to support non-driving activities." This came from the observation that drivers do all sorts of non-driving activities in their cars anyway. This reveals a gap: Automobiles have not been designed for how people actually use them in today's world. So, productivity features optimized for the safety of the driver will address an unmet need.

Let's see how this example looks when framed in the terms I've described in this, and the previous, chapter:

Cliché: Cars are for driving.

Hypothesis: What if cars were not for driving?

Insight: There's much more happening than just going for a drive, but cars are not designed to support non-driving activities. (Drivers currently use their cars to check email, make phone calls, and use their laptop.)

Opportunity: Help drivers [who] be more productive [advantage] in a way that's safe and optimized for driving [gap].

Describing the Opportunities

Remember that all of your research activities are done to drive the discovery of opportunities. It's possible that your opportunities may deviate from your original hypotheses as you work through this definition process. So, you might have to abandon or reframe your original hypotheses to sync them with your insights.

That's okay. Opportunities are totally context dependent. Too often, we assume that we correctly understand the context we're hypothesizing about and that all of our assumptions are correct. But, if you've discovered an insight that leads you in a completely different direction from where your hypotheses were taking you, go with it. That new direction may be just as valid, and perhaps more effective, because it's based on a better understanding of the context. Defining opportunities often requires a few backward or sideways steps now and then.

The important point is that your articulation of these opportunities should highlight an unexpected gap, a clear indication of an advantage, and a high-level reference to who it's for. Make sure it's customer focused.

After you describe your opportunity in one sentence, support your point of view with some key observations and insights from your research. For the car project, the team supported the "productivity" opportunity with the observation that, "Everyone thought it was a bad idea to be on the phone while driving, but they all did it anyway. A lot." They fleshed this out with even more observations, such as that drivers view car time as optimal time for making phone calls, and that when they're making those, they're generally alone, inside a controlled environment, and have "nothing else to do" (except drive, of course).

As a final example, let's go through the same process with the Swiffer mop: [17]

> **Cliché:** People use mops with water to clean floors.

> **Hypothesis:** What if mops did not use water?

> **Insight:** A common failure of cleaning floors is not a *lack* of water, but an *excess* of water. (Water slops dirt around.)

> **Opportunity:** Provide people at home [who] with a faster way to clean floors [advantage] without using water [gap].

Last point: An opportunity is not a solution. You've identified an advantage and a gap, but not the means of putting it into effect. Next, what you need are some ideas to execute the opportunity. That's the focus of Chapter 3.

Think Outside the Socks!
The Disruptive Opportunity

As I mentioned earlier, it's important to immerse yourself in the world of your customers, to try to see how things look from their viewpoint. And that's just what Jonah and his partners did. They had identified tween girls (ages 8–12) as their core target market, and by asking questions and paying close attention to the answers, they generated a number of observations which led to a key insight: Tween girls see themselves as being somewhere between a child and adult. They consider themselves sophisticated and mature, but they enjoy having fun and are still comfortable just being kids.

This insight suggested a disruptive opportunity—there were socks for kids and socks for adults, but nothing particularly compelling in between. The idea of wearing mismatched socks already sounded like self-expressive fun. If they could ensure that the socks also had a level of mature sophistication and premium quality, they could address a gap in the market.

Taking Action
(What Are Your Observations?)

Use the following list to plan your contextual research and gather your observations:

1. Determine the kinds of information you'd like to gather by making a list of questions.

2. Define the relevant audience: a mix of the target customer population, potential customers, and/or outlier customers.

3. Work out the timing required. Your decision will depend on the size and complexity of your focus, but it should be a rapid immersion: 2–3 hours for a quick informal study, 2–3 days for a longer one.

4. Set up interviews and observations in the context where people use the products and services that are relevant to your situation.

5. Allow for multiple observation sites so you'll be able to collect rich information across several environments.

6. Do at least two of the following:

   • **Open-ended Interview and observation:** Conduct on-site visits in each pre-arranged participant's place, whether it's a bank, an office, a supermarket, or a car wash. In addition to interviewing, make observations of the environments they live or work in. Look for implicit tension points in the form of workarounds to problems and the other points just listed. It is also important for you to understand the participant and the environment of the industry you are provoking. Recruit yourself or work with a recruiter,[18] develop a research plan, schedule visits, and conduct research.

- **Noninvasive observation:** Make observations in the context of people's interaction in public environments. How do people use computers, for example, at an airport gate while waiting for a flight? Unscheduled observations occur in a more ad-hoc manner. Determine your research questions, find locations where the activity takes place frequently, observe, and take photos or video.

- **Intercept:** Visit a store or public space that's relevant to your situation, watch the purchase process or general activities, and then approach and speak with people. When fellow customers ask whether someone had a good experience at the store, they often get a much different (and more accurate) answer than the one they would give to the checker (who would probably cheerfully ask, "Did you find everything you were looking for today?"). Your aim is to understand how people make decisions while in their normal flow of interaction with the relevant situation. Determine your research questions, find locations where the activity takes place frequently, approach participants, and ask questions.

Taking Action
(What Are Your Insights?)

Use the following list to organize your observations, make sense of your findings, and generate key insights:

1. Ground your data. Print or transcribe your observations, one per Post-It note. Print key photographs, sketches, or other images you collect.

2. Set up an insight board. Find a surface that's large enough for you to move, group, and arrange all of your observations and supporting information.

3. Cluster related observations and identify larger themes. Then, describe, in one or two words, the key theme that identifies each cluster. Write the name of the theme on a different colored Post-It note. For example, observations of how drivers use their cars to collect things, keep things handy for an extra side trip, and carry extra things to make a trip more comfortable, can form a theme for "being prepared."

4. Look for unexpected patterns. Start with the observations that surprise you and search for additional observations that suggest interrelated connections.

5. Generate insights by asking "why?" Interpret the patterns you see, using your best-guess intuition. Look for a counterintuitive rift between expectation and result. (For example, instead of removing dirt, water tends to slop it around.)

6. Capture your insights. Record them in real time and add them to your insight board. Keep going until you cover all of your themes. Aim for a minimum of one insight per theme.

7. Give your insights impact. Use paradoxical phrasing (but or whereas) to call attention to the gap exposed by the insight.

Taking Action (What Are Your Opportunities?)

Use the following list to organize your insights into opportunities, and then select one opportunity to pursue:

1. Match insights to your hypotheses. Which insights are related to which hypotheses?

2. Consider the relationship between insights and hypotheses. Look for the advantages that your insights suggest.

3. Group and re-group. Combine the insights in different ways to find the best hypothesis fit.

Use the following list to articulate the opportunity:

1. Describe the opportunity. You should be able to express each opportunity area in a three-part sentence. Confining your statement to one sentence focuses it on the expected advantages of the opportunity rather than the means of putting it into effect. (For example: The opportunity suggests that productivity features optimized for the safety of the driver will be an advantage. But, it stops short of

explaining what those productivity features will
be or how they'll be implemented.)

2. Provide the supporting logic. What are the key
   observations and insights from your research
   that make it obvious that the opportunity is
   advantageous? (For example: We observed
   that drivers currently make use of their vehicles for productivity, regardless of whether
   the in-car experience explicitly supports those
   activities or not.)

CHAPTER 3

Generating a Disruptive Idea:

Unexpected Ideas Have Fewer Competitors

"Imagination is more important than knowledge."
—Albert Einstein[1]

The Walt Disney Entertainment Company, one of the world's foremost storytellers, came to frog design a few years ago with a challenge. The company wanted to bring serious consumer electronics to their target demographic: *kids*. This was a disruptive hypothesis, because at the time, there weren't any consumer electronics for kids. Conventional industry wisdom always dredged up "My First Sony," which was an unsuccessful attempt by Sony to break into this market ten years earlier with a product that was too expensive, lacked breadth, and looked too much like a toy. "We tried that ten years ago, and it failed" is an anathema to anyone interested in disruptive thinking.

Industry observers had already dismissed this market segment as a dead end. But Disney is a content company, not a consumer-electronics company. Given its strong brand recognition, emotional resonance, and unique customer loyalty, Disney recognized that it was uniquely positioned to address this market in a different way. It sensed an opportunity to bring consumer electronics to life and infuse an entire line of products with Disney magic. The challenge went deeper than just slapping Mickey's face onto otherwise standard products. Disney wanted its brand association to be obvious, yet subtle.

But, opportunities by themselves don't lead to profits or lasting change. Disney needed to leverage its brand identity, integrate content elements, and expand the world of its beloved characters to create a usable *idea* that would emotionally resonate with kids and would have enough usable features to convince parents that they weren't buying yet another piece of junk. One of the first things we did was break down Disney's characters. We got books of all the most famous Disney films and cut out the eyes, hands, heads, and bodies of all the characters. We worked with a Disney animator to deconstruct the characters even further, carefully observing how they used basic components, like circles and lines, to give their characters personality and movement. After breaking them down like this, we noticed that there were definitely some patterns shared by characters—things most people never consciously notice.

Think about the perfect position of Mickey Mouse's ears: They never move, regardless of the position of his head, and that helps deliver a consistent silhouette. Or, the pervasive sense of asymmetry that gives characters a feel of constant movement, creating a sense of urgency and excitement.

Breaking down these patterns and thinking creatively about how we could connect them to consumer electronics laid the foundation for an entire product family, which is now distributed worldwide and generates $500 million in sales per year. Initially, we developed two products: a cordless phone and a two-way radio, both of which captured the essence of Disney characters without being too literal. For example, the mouthpiece of the phone looked like a smile and had a tiny lip line. The antenna took cues from Goofy's tail, and Donald Duck's eyes provided an analog for the design of the LCD display. It was all done very subtly, but when you held it in your hand, there was no question that it just felt like Disney.

As the Disney story shows, the big question for this chapter is: How do you transform an opportunity into an idea?

Transforming an Opportunity into an Idea

Well, the first thing is to get comfortable with the belief that any old ideas won't do. What we're interested in are disruptive ideas; that is, ideas with the power for great impact and influence. Ideas that challenge assumed boundaries and inspire a sense of what's possible. In my experience, however, most ideas never get anywhere near this level.

There are three major stumbling blocks:

1. Teams and individuals feel overwhelmed, directionless, and lack focus.

2. Many organizations still think of the world in terms of isolated products, services, and information.

3. Most ideas never get articulated in anything other than water-cooler conversations.

Let's look at all three stumbling blocks in more detail.

Stumbling Block 1
Teams and individuals feel overwhelmed, directionless, and lack focus.

In my experience, this is the direct result of relying on traditional brainstorming approaches, which, by the way, have been around since the 1930s, when ad-man Alex Faickney Osborn first popularized them in his book, *Applied Imagination*. Osborn proposed that groups could double their creative output with brainstorming, but he placed little emphasis on how to focus creative thinking and refine the quality of the output. The brainstorming method relies on participants saying anything that comes to mind, in response to a loosely defined focus, with the hope that something might just prove useful.

On its face, that sounds reasonable. But, the problem is that traditional brainstorming has ignored the huge difference between generating lots of ideas and capturing *quality* ideas. As a result, brainstorming sessions often leave organizations and teams feeling overwhelmed and directionless—a state Beth Comstock at GE insightfully calls, "paralyzed by possibility."[2] Simply put, if your ideas are going to have any disruptive impact, you need to move beyond a shotgun approach to brainstorming and start pursuing creative effort with a laser-sharp focus.

Stumbling Block 2
Many organizations still think of the world in terms of isolated products, services, and information.

This is a mistake. They should be thinking more holistically of product-service-information hybrids.

It's getting harder and harder to compete if you don't. The real advantage comes when your disruptive idea is blended in such a way that the product, service, and information components can't be broken apart.[3] For example, the disruptive idea behind the iPhone is that it blends product (e.g., iPhone with iPhone OS), service (iTunes+App Store), and information from the network (which includes wireless providers, Google, Yahoo!, iPhone developers, related iPhone social networks and communities, and the manufacturers).

To get a better sense of what I'm talking about, consider this quote from Bruce Sterling's *Shaping Things*: "...this Sangiovese may be a 'classic' wine from the Mediterranean basin, but this bottle is no longer a classic artifact. It has been gizmo-ized."

Gizmo-ized is another way of saying that even a product as ancient as a bottle of wine no longer stands alone as a static object; it's dynamic. "It is offering me more functionality than I will ever be able to explore," Sterling writes, "This wine bottle aims to educate me—it is luring me to become more knowledgeable about the people and processes that made the bottle and its contents. It wants to recruit me to become an unpaid promotional agent, a wine critic, an opinion maker—it wants me to throw wine-tasting parties and tell all my friends about my purchase."[4]

In Sterling's view, there is nothing frivolous or extraneous about this sudden explosion of informational intimacy between himself (with his laptop), and a bottle of wine (with its website): "My relationship with this bottle of wine is a parable of my human relationship to all objects."[5] It enables a deeper, more intimate relationship between consumers and producers.

Clearly, we need a new mindset when it comes to generating ideas: one focused on the dynamics of a blended whole, rather than the details of its isolated parts. In other words, the relationship between a product, a service, and the information they provide is more important than the details of any one particular feature alone.

That said, don't slip into thinking of disruptive ideas only in relation to new gadgets and technology. You can develop disruptive ideas for any opportunity you desire.

Stumbling Block 3
Most ideas never get articulated in anything other than water-cooler conversations.

As a result, they rarely escape people's heads and instead remain there, unformed. The view from inside the company, however, is different. One of the most common phrases I hear from clients is, "We don't need any more ideas; we have too many." But when I ask to see the documented ideas they have, they start back-pedaling: "Well, we don't have them written down or anything. But, we discuss them a lot."

That's the problem in a nutshell. You can talk about ideas in general terms, at least for a while. However, abstraction makes it harder to understand an idea and remember it. So, to increase the potential, you have to stop talking about it and explain it in sensory terms. "Sketch it out!," as Hartmut Esslinger, founder of frog design, used to say. (He wouldn't listen to an idea if you hadn't done so.) Ambiguity disappears when you describe your ideas in visual or written form.

Getting past these three stumbling blocks is a challenge. The chaos of a creative process is over-whelming. It's easier to think in terms of isolated products, services, and information, rather than blended hybrids. And, it takes considerably less effort to vaguely talk about ideas rather than specifically describe and visualize them.

This is where the methods in this chapter come into play. They will help you move past these stumbling blocks and generate the kind of disruptive ideas that transform compelling opportunities into commercial offerings.

What Is Your Focus?
(Getting Past Stumbling Block 1)

In the beginning of Chapter 2, I talked about how Apple progressed from

- Observation (people in Mac stores like to touch the computers) to…

- Insight (you're rarely intimidated by something you want to touch, and if you're intimidated, you don't want to touch it) to…

- Opportunity (provide people a sense of control over the technology by establishing an immediate physical connection between the user and the computer).

To say there's an opportunity "to provide customers with a sense of control by establishing an immediate physical connection" is wonderful, but it doesn't do anything by itself. We need specific ways to accomplish that goal. Remember: Hypotheses feed observations. Observations feed insights. Insights feed opportunities. *Opportunities feed ideas.*

Hypotheses feed observations. Observations feed insights. Insights feed opportunities. *Opportunities feed ideas.*

Focus Your Creative Effort

At this point, you should have identified and described an opportunity. Now, it's time to develop the ideas to execute it. You'll start by breaking down your opportunity into a number of parts and examining each one in a new way. It doesn't matter if you don't get to all of them. The main point is to focus your creativity.

In Chapter 2, I used the opportunity identified for a car manufacturer: "Provide drivers [*who*] with ways of being more productive [*advantage*] that are safe and optimized for driving [*gap*]."

Now for the breakdown. Start by focusing on one area of an opportunity statement: the *advantage*. (Opportunity statements can often seem overwhelming, so starting with one small piece will make it easier to work with.) The advantage, in this case, is "productivity." Then, ask yourself when drivers could make use of their vehicles for productivity.

You might come up with something like this:

When running errands

When making phone calls

When dealing with inspiration (taking notes, for example)

When waiting (at lights, in traffic)

When traveling with kids (entertainment)

There are no "right" or "wrong" breakdowns. And we aren't trying to come up with a comprehensive breakdown. That's way too analytical for our purposes and, given how many possibilities there are, I'm not sure it's even possible. The goal is simply to hone your focus and get those creative juices flowing.

After you have the advantage part of the opportunity broken down, you can start asking yourself all sorts of questions about how to deliver on the *gap* part of the opportunity. Again consider our car example. The gap part of the opportunity statement is "safe and optimized" for driving. So, some of the questions might be:

How can we safely optimize the way people make phone calls in their car?

Idea: Integrated hands free phone calls.

How can we safely optimize the way people take notes in their car?

Idea: Hazard avoidance systems.

How can we safely optimize the way people entertain their kids in their car?

Idea: Integrated DVD players.

After you have the opportunity broken down into questions like these, try to answer them with as many new ideas as you can think of—from the obvious to the ridiculous. And be sure not to reject any ideas too quickly. That's usually the result of applying some real-world constraints to the situation. ("That won't work because…we don't have the money, or the resources, or the capacity.") You'll have plenty of time to evaluate your ideas later. But for now, stay focused on generating them. And if you need an extra dose of inspiration, check out the next step.

Forcing Connections

It's always a good tactic to look for examples of how a particular advantage or gap has been addressed in products or services outside of the situation you're focused on.[6] Because the problem is that most easily conceived ideas are the most familiar ones, the ones you've experienced most often. As a result, more often than not, the first ideas out of people's mouths are stale clichés—and the fundamental sin of any disruptive idea is for it to be a cliché. It reminds me of Robert McKee's advice to would-be film makers: "Cliché is at the root of audience dissatisfaction…. Too often we close novels or exit theaters bored by an ending that was obvious from the beginning, disgruntled because we've seen these cliché scenes and characters too many times before."[7] McKee could just as accurately be describing the first ideas to arise from a typical brainstorming session in a corporate boardroom.

To break away from cliché-thinking, you need to develop a habit of looking for alternative ideas instead of immediately accepting the most obvious approaches. Inspiration for break-through ideas often happens in the periphery, in analogous but not necessarily traditionally competitive categories. The next time you're sweetening your coffee with Sweet'N Low, consider that the only reason it's touching your lips is because a chemist working on coal tar derivatives made an unexpected discovery: the artificial sweetener *saccharin*. The goal is to look closely at the unconnected example and figure out how you could apply the entire idea, or part of it, to your needs. As *New York Times* columnist and author Thomas Friedman puts it, "The further we push out the boundaries of knowledge and innovation, the more the next great value breakthroughs—that is, the next new hot-selling products and services—will come from putting together disparate things that you would never think of as going together." [8]

For example, a door handle is a physical connection between a person and a building. How could that relate to establishing a physical connection between a person and a computer? Apple's solution was to put a handle on the iMac so that it's the first thing people see when they take it out of the box. And grabbing the computer by the handle gives them an immediate sense of control over the technology. This is a powerful exercise, because it's possible that you could take an idea that was developed in a completely unrelated field and directly apply it to your situation. Think back to the Nintendo Wii and the handheld controller that integrates the movements of a player directly into the video game. The inspiration for the motion controller idea didn't come from looking at what other video consoles were doing; it came from a completely unrelated source: the accelerometer chip that regulates the airbag in your car. Airbags respond to sudden changes in movement caused by accidents. Nintendo wondered if it would be possible to combine the accelerometer used by airbags with a handheld controller used to play video games. In other words, if you swung the controller like a tennis racket, could a "virtual you" on the screen swing as well? [9]

Nintendo combined the accelerometer used by airbags with a hand-held controller used to play video games.

Here's another example of how bringing two seemingly unrelated thoughts together sparked a new way of seeing things. One morning, a designer sprang into the frog design studio with a little more energy than usual.

"I know why everyone says the iPod looks clean!," he exclaimed. The iPod has become—in the minds of most of our clients and just about everyone else in the world—the poster product of great innovation. Ask anyone to tell you what they find so appealing about the design of the iPod, and, almost without exception, they answer, "I like it because it looks clean."

Of course, there are obvious clues, such as the minimalist design; the simple, intuitive interface; and the neutral colors. But, these attributes alone don't fully explain this seemingly universal perception of graceful hygiene. There had to be something deeper. And if a designer claimed that he had the answer, we were all ears.

"So," the visiting designer said, "as I was sitting on the toilet this morning (which, of course, is where most good ideas come from), I noticed the shiny white porcelain of the bathtub and the reflective chrome of the faucet on the wash basin... and then it hit me! Everybody perceives the iPod as 'clean' because it references bathroom materials."

There were a few seconds of silence...followed quickly by enthusiastic laughter. No, not because he had arrived at this insight by sitting on the toilet. We were laughing because we knew that Jonathan Ive, who designed the iPod, came to Apple from a London-based design consultancy where he worked on a lot of lavatory basins.[10]

Coincidence? Perhaps. But, at the very least, it's an example of how anything, no matter how unconnected, can spark new perceptions. Often, the more incompatible the connection, the more useful it may be—and the more it can help you break away from cliché-thinking and cultivate a fresh perspective. In the words of serial entrepreneur, Marc Andreessen, "The freshness of an idea can be tested by how much ridicule it provokes. An idea that isn't ridiculed is probably stale."[11]

What Can You Blend Together? (Getting Past Stumbling Block 2)

Before we move on, let's quickly look at the ideas you've generated for your opportunity. Going through the exercise in the first part of this chapter should have produced a dozen ideas.

Not all the ideas you've generated will be worth pursuing, so pick the three that you think are the most promising. In other words, the three that offer the greatest differentiation and the largest number of benefits to either your customers or your company. Why three? Because three gives you a good range to experiment, challenge assumptions, and gather feedback in the next stage.

These are usually the ideas that you and everyone on your team (if you're working in a team) recognizes as sure winners. Others aren't nearly as good, and everyone might agree that they're unworkable.

A word of caution: Don't worry about trying to select the most practical ideas; focus on the most disruptive ones. We'll work on developing the practical ones in the next stage of the process (see Chapter 4). In the meantime, try to look past the obvious, and be sure to consider some ideas you aren't sure about and that are unusual enough to be disruptive.

Many significant innovations in the last century got their start as unexpected discoveries or seemingly impractical ideas. One of the most famous of these occurred in 1928 when Scottish Scientist Alexander Fleming was researching the flu and noticed that a blue-green mold had infected one of his Petri dishes and killed the staphylococcus bacteria growing in it. The result? Penicillin.

Many significant innovations got their start as unexpected discoveries or impractical ideas.

Refine Three Ideas

After you select your three ideas, start the process of refining them into a more holistic and powerful form.

The stumbling block here is that many organizations still think of their offerings to customers as isolated products, services, and information. When they do think of these components together, companies tend to use the word *bundle*, which still has the connotation of separate products. But, as I mentioned, real meaning comes when an offering is blended in such a way that the product, service, and information components can't succeed independently.

Two blending techniques are especially helpful (they're the two I use when working with clients):

- **Blend the bits.** Start thinking about the product, service, and information bits simultaneously. So, if one of your ideas is for a new product, what are the services and networked information that would be essential in supporting that product?

  For example, the phone we developed for Disney started as an idea for a cordless phone that rests in a charging base that looks like Mickey's shoe (the product). We then added a way for people to find misplaced handsets. By pressing a button on the charging base, Mickey's voice would scream, "I'm over here!" (information). This then led us to think about "downloadable character voices" so Donald Duck and Goofy could tell you where they are, too (the service).

- **Blend the benefits.** Always remember that, with few exceptions, whatever you're offering has to benefit three key customers: partners, buyers, and users. What are the benefits? Whom do they benefit? How and under what circumstances are they delivered? If only one or two of those customer groups actually reaps the benefits, try to even things out. Otherwise, your offer may end up too lopsided to be successful.

The new media brand Hulu, for example, does a great job of recognizing that it has three types of customers, and it makes every benefit decision in a balanced way. According to CEO Jason Kilar, "I'm not saying it's easy, but we constantly live that delicate balance between our three customers and not sacrificing one out of the three or two out of the three. If you ever stop by the office, I think you'd feel that advertiser focus. You'd feel that user focus and you'd feel that content provider focus."[12]

Likewise, the Disney offering needed to deliver benefits to the partners (retailers), the buyers (parents), and the users (kids) at every point where a customer could possibly interact with it. Take, for example, the point of purchase.

For the kids, the benefit was seeing their favorite characters on the packaging and being able to interact with the boxes and products at their height. That sounds obvious, but standard shelving units (in anything other than a toy store) are too high for kids. For parents, it was learning about how multiple components worked together. For example, the products shipped with two remotes: the one for the kids had very few buttons, while the one for parents was as functional as most standard remotes. We conveyed this benefit by creating a looped DVD reel that demonstrated 16 different products in action as used by a family. All of this helped retailers achieve one of the highest "attachment rates" of TV and DVD player sales in the industry, meaning that parents bought them together instead of separately—a real rarity in consumer electronics.

Your search for benefits should take into consideration how the ideas will be implemented (through existing channels and operations?), and the consequences of implementation (will the full benefits come through in months, years, or decades?). Consider also when and where the idea will be used. What will happen at those key touch-points in the short term, medium term, and long term?

Write down every possible benefit you can come up with—not just the obvious ones. And be prepared to make some changes to make those benefits more obvious.

What Are Your Disruptive Ideas? (Getting Past Stumbling Block 3)

Talking about ideas—as opposed to documenting them—keeps them general and abstract. And an abstract idea is harder to understand and remember—both for you and anyone else you might want to share it with. Showing ideas, on the other hand, makes them specific and concrete, which in turn, makes them easy to share, understand, and remember.

So, after you refine your three ideas by blending the bits and the benefits, you need to create a one-page or slide overview of each idea, accurately describing it in words and pictures. If you decide you want to further develop an idea into a solution for the market, having documented your ideas in this way will make it easier to get critical feedback from consumers. Use the following list as a guide for putting together your one-pager.

- **Name:** Giving your idea a name is the first step toward making it concrete and easily graspable by others. Pick a name that accurately represents the idea and makes it stand out. It should be short, memorable, and credible. Finally, make it easy to pronounce and easy on the ears when it's spoken. Look to the marketplace and examples of your favorite brands for inspiration: *BlackBerry, PayPal, Under Armor, FedEx.* All strong names.

To make the name of your idea stand out, remember that people have a better chance of remembering something unique than something common; that's just the way our memory works. So, once you have a name that you think accurately represents the idea, give it a twist—deliberately misspell it, mess with the grammar, collapse two words together, or add additional letters. Quentin Tarantino did this with his 2009 movie *Inglorious Basterds*.

If you need a little guidance on naming, there's plenty to learn from the movie industry. Consultant and former MGM Executive Stephanie Palmer once asked a client, "Can you imagine seeing a movie called *3,000 Dollars*? Can you identify the genre?"[13] According to Stephanie, that was the original title of *Pretty Woman*, and the $3,000 was the fee Julia Roberts' character charged for her services.

Although you can't overestimate the power of a great name, don't spend an inordinate amount of time on it. We're not talking about a public-facing brand, so 10–15 minutes should be plenty of time. Right now, the name's sole purpose is to help the people you share it with understand and remember it.

- **Describe:** The next step is to concisely describe the central message you want to communicate. How concise? One sentence. You want to capture the following:

  - What it is (label).

  - Whom it's for (user).

- Why they should care (benefit).

- How your idea will deliver that benefit (method).

When you're ready to try putting together your description, use this template:

A _____ [label] that allows _____ [user] to _____ [benefit] by _____ [method].

Let's examine the four components of the one-sentence description in more detail. (And yes, I see the irony in taking two pages to describe how to craft one sentence.)

- **Label:** The label you assign to your idea refers to the category the idea will be associated with, and how broad or narrow you want that association to be. A label is a trigger feature—that is, when people encounter a new idea, they have a tendency to respond in terms of what they already know. The label you give an idea cues people toward a particular set of associations. For example, imagine that you've got a new idea for how people can clean their teeth. You could use either "toothbrush" or "oral care device" as a label. The difference is significant.

  "Toothbrush" is specific and carries a hard-edged association, so everything that you're presenting about your new idea for "cleaning teeth" is now filtered through the listener's mental image of how a toothbrush should look, function, be used, priced, sold, distributed, and so on. On the other hand, the label "oral care device" is broader and carries a wider set of associations (mouthwash, floss, whitening strips, and so on). A toothbrush may pop into people's minds, but they'll generally be more open to alternative ways of thinking about the cleaning of teeth.

- **User:** Although this solution may benefit many different groups (such as producers, buyers, and suppliers), who is the primary end user or consumer you're trying to reach?

- **Benefit:** What's the one key benefit that the user derives from the solution you're proposing?

- **Method:** This refers to the specific ways your solution will deliver the benefit. A toothbrush, for example, is a handle with a head of bristles that holds toothpaste.

Coming up with a one-sentence description is more complicated than it sounds. One great way to give yourself a little practice is to spend some time looking closely at the products and services you see every day. Try to extract the four components and describe them in one sentence.

Example: A digital music system that allows people on the move to carry 1,000 songs in their pocket by synchronizing a portable device with an online music store. (*iPod*)

Example. A point-and-shoot video camera that allows anyone with Internet access to figure out, in seconds, how to record and share videos with low-quality footage and stripped-down features. (*Flip Ultra*)

To refine your description, ask yourself, "Could this describe anything else?" If the answer is yes, your description is too generic. Look for ways to further customize it to your idea. It's usually not a matter of making the description longer. Instead, look to make each of the four terms in the sentence more specific.

- **Differentiate:** It's important that you emphasize the differences between your disruptive idea and any competing offerings that may be floating around in the same industry or context. But, being different isn't enough. Your idea must be different in ways that are valued by and relevant to potential customers. Being different means making tradeoffs in the features and functionality of your disruptive idea.

Here's how journalist Robert Capps describes the tradeoffs that Pure Digital had to make to differentiate its Flip cameras from other camcorders:

> It captured relatively low-quality 640 x 480 footage at a time when Sony, Panasonic, and Canon were launching camcorders capable of recording in 1080 hi-def. It had a minuscule viewing screen, no color-adjustment features, and only the most rudimentary controls. It didn't even have an optical zoom. But it was small (slightly bigger than a pack of smokes), inexpensive ($150, compared with $800 for a midpriced Sony), and so simple to operate—from recording to uploading—that pretty much anyone could figure it out in roughly 6.7 seconds.[14]

As it turned out, these differences were highly valued by customers. Pure Digital sold more than a million units in the first year and quickly captured 17 percent of the camcorder market. In the years since, Sony, Canon, Panasonic, Kodak, and others have come out with similar cameras.

- **Visualize:** The old saying that a picture is worth a thousand words is just as true in simple situations as it is in complex ones. Try, for example, to describe the physical process for filling a water glass. Even the most basic systems quickly start sounding awkward.[15] "When I fill a glass of water, there is a feedback process that causes me to adjust the faucet position, which adjusts the water flow and alters the water level. The goal of the process is to make the water in the glass rise to my desired level."

A drawing of the system, or a visual representation of the process, is much easier to digest.

Consider the process of making a movie. Sure, a script provides a verbal summary of events. But, the storyboard that goes along with the script is far more powerful and efficient. Simple pictures and sketches of each key scene communicate to a diverse set of people working on the set. One simple picture can provide direction to dozens of cast and crewmembers. It can show the set designers what to create, the camera crew where to position the camera, the costume designers what to design, and the actors how to relate.

Your disruptive idea needs to be visual to concretely describe its components, features, and functionality; in other words, how does it work? For example, if you have an idea for a new set of music headphones with a retractable microphone for cell phone use, you need to show people how it would be worn and used. It is not enough just to list features. Visualizing how your idea works ensures that everyone you show it to will see it the same way.

Elizabeth Diller, New York architect and co-founder of Diller Scofidio and Renfro, once advised a student, "It's not enough to say the screens will show digital information." This leaves matters at a far-too-general level. 'What digital information will they show?'"[16]

One final word of advice: Don't worry about getting your visualization perfect or let yourself get locked-in to whatever details you've included. The details you give when you visualize your concepts aren't necessarily in their final form. In the next stage, we'll run your idea through all sorts of refinements and changes. But at this stage of the process, any visualization—no matter how rough or approximate—is better than none.

Think Outside the Socks!
The Disruptive Idea

Having discovered the opportunity, Jonah and his partners needed to generate some ideas for how to brand and sell mismatched socks. They broke the opportunity down and started with the challenge of how to stand out in a crowded market. Jonah knew from his experience with consumer product retailers that corporate buyers have different price points for similar products. Items classified as "licensed" (think Disney, Nike, Dell, Harley-Davidson) command a higher price than products classified as "general merchandise" (think generics and store brands).

In Jonah's mind, there was no reason this same logic couldn't work for socks. This led to the idea of creating a catchy name and a character that would appeal to tweens and set the brand apart from the clutter. They came up with several other ways of setting their new brand apart from the generic competition. Perhaps the most important was the idea that the socks shouldn't be packaged and sold in the traditional way. Socks sold in pairs are expected to match. What would suggest that the socks intentionally did not match? *Socks sold in sets of three.*

As we talked about in this chapter, sketching things out is critical. In this case, they needed to get down on paper a vision of the brand's character and what the mismatched socks would look like. They sketched a graphic of Little Miss Matched herself— a tween girl with a knowing smirk—that became the face of the brand. To help visualize the mismatched socks, one of the partners created a versatile color and pattern palette that was both fun and sophisticated. She then created watercolor drawings of 133 style combinations, with none of them matching (but, because of the clever palette, they all looked good together).

Taking Action

Use the following list to generate ideas for the opportunity you defined in the previous stage:

Breakdown

To break down the opportunity and generate ideas, go through the following steps:

1. Note the *advantage* part of the opportunity statement; then list 4–5 moments for *when* this advantage could be addressed.

2. Note the *gap* part of the opportunity statement; then think about *how* this could be addressed for each of the *when* moments.

3. Think creatively about answers to each question, and generate as many new ideas as you can.

4. For inspiration, look for examples of how a particular *advantage* or *gap* has been addressed in products or services outside of your industry and situation.

5. Figure out how to connect the outside idea to your situation.

Blend

For each idea, go through the following two steps to refine the offering:

1. **Blend the bits:** Consider the product, service, and information bits simultaneously to create a hybrid offering.

2. **Blend the benefits:** Consider the benefits being offered to partners, buyers, and users.

Articulate

Follow these steps to create a one-pager for each disruptive idea:

1. Give your idea a name. Make it short and memorable.

2. Craft a one-sentence description to briefly describe what the idea is and why it's important. Include four key components: label, user, benefit, and method.

3. Describe how it's different. Include one significant point and several minor ones.

4. Create an annotated visualization of your idea that concretely shows its components, features, and functionality. You can use any or all of the following: hand-drawn sketch, Photoshop montage, diagram, video, or system map.

That brings us to the end of Part I. If you've followed the process so far, you should have three disruptive ideas—ideas that have potential but still need to be tested and refined. If you want to take those ideas to the next level, Part II will get you there, walking you through the process of gaining consumer feedback, transforming your idea into a solution, and then pitching the results.

PART II

The Solution and the Pitch

CHAPTER 4

Shaping a Disruptive Solution:

Novelty for Novelty's Sake Is a Resource Killer

"Your company's chance of creating new wealth is
directly proportional to the number of ideas it fosters
and the number of experiments it starts. So ask
yourself, 'How diverse is your company's portfolio of
unconventional strategy options?'"
—Gary Hamel[1]

One of frog design's clients, a major beauty-products
manufacturer, came to us looking for a way to extend
one of its most successful products, a microderm abrasion skin rejuvenation kit, which was aimed at older
women. The company's idea was to combine microderm abrasion technology with its skin-cleanser line
and create a new handheld product aimed at a younger
crowd. They came to frog design to help them design
the new product.

Initially, the client targeted its new offering at women 25–45, but after we tested that initial hypothesis, we discovered that the real opportunity was with the tween-to-early 20s demographic. Because buyers of most of the company's products were typically older than that, even considering marketing to younger consumers meant understanding a new market.

We began by deeply immersing ourselves in the habits and behavior of typical customers of skincare and personal-health devices. By doing extensive interviews and in-home observations, we came to understand how skincare rituals fit into young women's daily lives and physical environments. We also discovered that nearly every woman—rich or poor, living in a tiny studio apartment or a huge suburban mansion—had a box somewhere in her house filled with unused or underused skincare and healthcare products.

These observations yielded a set of insights, which our designers used to generate a number of exciting ideas around color, form, and materials. At least they *seemed* exciting to our design team, which consisted of a handful of talented, 30-something men and women. There wasn't a single teen girl in the bunch—and that was a problem.

Disruptive ideas are great, but they're only half the story. Unless those ideas can be made feasible, they can't deliver value. How do you know whether an idea is feasible? Well, you don't—unless you actually see how it plays with your target market. Without testing our ideas with prospective end users and consumers, we were in danger of coming up with some really terrific ideas that would completely flop when they hit store shelves.

Let me give another example: The Edsel has earned a place in marketing lore as perhaps one of the biggest corporate blunders of the past few centuries.[2] The story has been hashed and rehashed in countless articles and business-school case studies. But there's one aspect of the story that doesn't get much attention: the Teletouch, a push-button automatic transmission interface that was located in the center of the steering wheel. A beautiful, innovative design, no doubt. But Ford's engineers were working in a secretive bubble and wouldn't let anyone see or interact with the new car. As a result, when the car was finally released and people actually had a chance to test-drive it, they absolutely hated that every time they wanted to honk their horn, they accidentally shifted gears. We'll talk more about the Edsel later, but suffice it to say here, that's the kind of thing that happens when designers and end users are kept away from each other.

Drivers hated that every time they wanted to honk their horn, they accidentally shifted gears.

In this chapter, we change our focus from conceiving ideas to turning those ideas into practical solutions. The difference between an idea and a solution is that the latter is always feasible. If it's not, it's not really a solution. At the end of the previous chapter, you generated three disruptive ideas, which may or may not be practical. By the time you're done with this chapter, you'll have refined one or more of those ideas into something that's truly workable.

The best way to get from disruptive idea to practical solution is to actively involve end users to test and review. I know that may sound like a traditional focus group, but it's not. Participants actually become part of a collaborative, creative process. Of course, you have a far greater understanding of the project than they do, but they're still a critical reality check. They're now the experts, and you're not behind the glass in another room observing. You're working together, not only to evaluate and validate ideas, but also to work on improvements. In a very real sense, you're co-creating a solution.

To get from disruptive idea to practical solution, actively involve end users to test and review.

Why is this important? Because, as the story of Teletouch gearshift illustrates, it's not enough just to come up with something disruptive; it has to be disruptive in ways that are valued by users. Novelty for novelty's sake is an indulgence and a waste of resources.

In the second part of the chapter, we'll talk about how to synthesize the information and feedback you get from consumers into a tangible prototype of your solution. (And yes, even services have a tangible component, which we'll discuss in detail.)

What Do People Really Think? (As Opposed to What They Tell You They're Thinking)

Facilitating feedback from prospective end users is a critical component of the process because it can reveal the gaps between what you claim you want to accomplish with your idea and what you are actually willing (or able) to do. It may also reveal that those ideas you thought were so disruptive aren't really so hot after all. Better to find that out right now than after you've sunk a ton of money into implementation. There are three basic ways of recruiting consumers for research. First, you could hire one of the many companies that do this kind of thing professionally. You give them a list of the characteristics you're looking for (more on that later). They then go through their databases and come up with a large group of likely prospects, whom they prescreen, screen, weed out, and eventually give you a solid shortlist.

Second, if you haven't got the budget (and, believe me, the professional route is not cheap), you can go guerilla and find your own participants by posting ads on online bulletin boards, such as Craig's List.

Third, you could tap into your network of friends and family. Although this is definitely the cheapest way to go, I don't often recommend it, in part because of what you might call "the mom effect." That's when people (like your mom) tell you that all of your ideas are great just the way they are. And you're cute, too. This kind of feedback is useless. Because the professional option isn't a possibility for many companies, let's talk about how the guerilla method works.

Your first order of business is to come up with a description of the kind of person you think is your target consumer. (You'd do this step when working with professional recruiters or identifying family and friends, too.) In our microderm abrasion example, that company was looking for females age 12–24 who

- Had used some kind of microderm abrasion (MDA) kit, either made by our client or a competitor, or had visited a dermatologist for MDA or other facial treatment

- Owned at least one MDA kit

Then, you craft a short ad and post it on Craig's List or another similar site. You want to be provocative yet vague. For example, "Are you a female between the ages of 12 and 25? Are you interested in participating in the design process for a new skincare product?"

Chances are, you'll get a flood of responses. Eliminate the ones that are obviously inappropriate (the people who clearly didn't read your ad and think you're hiring telemarketers, the ones who want to sell you something that will expand various parts of your anatomy, and anyone else who's completely off base). That should leave you with a pool of about 20–30 people.

Next, conduct email follow-ups. After a few rounds of email questions, you should be able to narrow the pool to about a dozen potential subjects. Now, it's time to pick up the phone and make your final choices. Keep in mind that this isn't about putting together a huge, statistically significant sample. It's about generating rich insights and exploring nuances in detail. Ideally, you'll hone your choices to nine participants: three teams of three. If you can't get to nine, six will pass. If you absolutely have to, three will do in a pinch. But, don't go lower than that.

The microderm abrasion project required a group of highly experienced and engaged subjects. Here's what the final nine looked like:

- They responded in a timely way to our email communications (all).

- They answered product questions quickly (all).

- Worked full time (at least 3).

- Worked part time (at least 3).

- Had visited a dermatologist for MDA and facial-related treatments (2).

- Had a history of microderm abrasion use (all; professional 2).

- Owned one of our client's MDA kits (3).

- Owned a competitor's kit (all).

- Had used two or more MDA systems (4).

- Had positive results with MDA systems (4).

- Had negative results (at least 2).

After you finalize your participants, bring them into your office (or wherever you'll be doing the testing), where, over the next few hours, you'll run them through the following five activities[3] (we'll discuss each one in detail):

1. Memory mapping

2. Individual ranking

3. Group ranking

4. Improvement exercise

5. Open discussion

Memory Mapping

After a brief introduction where you tell the participants about the project, you'll ask them to think about the situation you're focused on and draw—from memory—the product or service they currently use. This technique won't give you a reliable indication of consumers' preferences or purchase intentions. But you're not using it for that, anyway.

If you're planning on introducing a marketplace disruption, you need to know what your customers' mental models are and whether your solution violates their "rules" for how they think it should be used. Asking your participants to verbally describe a product or service won't do the job. Having them physically draw it out (even in the most rudimentary way) is critical. You need to see how it's laid out, how it functions, and how they see it in action. That way, if any of the participants say they hate your idea, you'll have a much better idea *why*.

Problems happen when there's a disconnect between your end user's mental model and yours. Designers know a lot about how their new ideas will work, but little about how people will actually interact with them. Conversely, end users know how they will (or would like to) interact with things, but not much about how you'd like to have them work.

Just to be clear, I'm not saying that you should never violate your consumers' rules or mental models. Not at all. The point I'm making is that breaking models is actually a good thing—as long as you have a compelling reason for doing so. Imagine that one of your disruptive ideas is a new remote control with the power button in the lower left corner. If all of your participants drew remotes with power buttons in the upper right, you'll know that if you insist on the lower left placement, you're going to need a much better reason than, "It looks kinda cool there." If you don't have one, you've got no business trying to change anyone's mental models.

A participant drawing a product from memory.

To reach a feasible solution, you need to balance the magic, mystery, and creative intuition that lead you to your disruptive ideas with the messy, real, unpredictable pressures of the market. In other words, you need to close the loop between the end user's mental model and yours. If Edsel's engineers would have asked people to draw an automatic transmission gear shifter, they would have gotten pictures of steering-column levers or four-on-the-floor. They would have known that they were breaking an important rule and might have reconsidered their plan to put push buttons in the center of the steering wheel where the horn usually goes. (But again, just because an idea violates a mental model is not always a justification for tossing it. We'll talk about this later.)

Individual Ranking

Before you conduct this exercise, you should have a clear idea of the attributes that you expect your solution to have. For example, the attributes we used for our client were

- Elegant

- Clear

- Affordable

- Special

- Fun

As you can see, these values are extremely broad. Write all of your attributes in a column on a sheet of paper with a 1–5 scale next to each one. Give one of these worksheets to each participant.

Then, introduce your ideas, one at a time, to the participants as a group. Ask them to refrain from commenting while they're listening, and then ask participants to rate the ideas according to the attributes on the worksheet you just gave them, with 1 being the lowest grade and 5 the highest. On the same sheet, ask them to summarize their first impressions of the idea. You'll go through this sequence for each disruptive idea. (You'll need separate worksheets for each idea; the attributes remain the same.)

The important thing to remember about this exercise is that it must be a 100-percent individual effort. Participants should not discuss their ratings or talk about what they're writing. Having them individually rate the ideas really cuts down on groupthink and follow-the-leader mentality. The more comments like, "I agree with Bob...," the less helpful the results.

After all the participants finish their individual worksheets, open up the discussion and encourage them to talk about their reactions to the ideas. Then, have them return to the sheets and write down how/whether their impressions have changed.

Participants individually rating ideas.

Group Ranking

After a little group discussion, you'll give each three-person team a new worksheet. This one will have a list of attributes in a column down the left edge of the paper. For example:

- Elegant

- Clear

- Affordable

- Special

- Fun

Down the right edge, you'll list the polar opposites. For example:

- Cute

- Confusing

- Expensive

- Plain

- Serious

Between the two columns, you'll leave one short blank line for each idea. The blank sheet will look something like this:

Elegant	_____ _____ _____	Cute
Clear	_____ _____ _____	Confusing
Affordable	_____ _____ _____	Expensive
Special	_____ _____ _____	Plain
Fun	_____ _____ _____	Serious

Now, give each team a sheet of colored dots—one color per idea—and ask them to work together to order the ideas in relation to each other within each of the polar categories.

Your task here is to facilitate a discussion in which the participants negotiate with each other to determine where the dots should go. You want to hear their arguments and their reasoning. But most of all, you want them to try to convince each other and come to a final decision as a group. Having spent some time thinking about the ideas individually should reduce the amount of leader following that goes on. It's kind of like going out refrigerator shopping with a family member. Each of you will point out to each other things the other hadn't seen.

The final step is to get the participants to come up with a favorite overall choice.

Participants working together to rank ideas.

Improvement Exercise

After getting individual and group feedback on each of your ideas from your participants, the next activity is to bring them into the process of constructively improving those ideas. Our goal here is to hone the range of ideas you started with into one practical, workable direction.

Looking at the arrangement of the dots in the previous step, you may see that there's one clear winner, one idea that scored at the top on nearly every attribute. If that doesn't happen (and it's generally rare), don't worry. The solution is to create a hybrid: a single idea that incorporates the best features of each of the three options your group participants have evaluated.

Every time I run this exercise, whether it's running workshops, teaching MBA students, or working with clients, I've found that the group participants really get into it, especially if they're encouraged to think of themselves as integral to the creative process and not simply being focused grouped or interviewed.

Open Discussion

Now that your participants have thought about and played with your disruptive ideas, and they have a good sense of how the various attributes could impact them, this is the perfect time to take 15 minutes or so to ask them about value. The best way to do this is to come right out and ask them, "How much would you pay for this product or service?" There's no other way to find out what that is than to inquire. Even though you're asking for numbers, you're not actually going to use this information to set the price of the offering. You're gauging their level of enthusiasm.

Before you send everyone home with their thank-you gifts, take one last moment to summarize what they liked and didn't like about each idea.

As you mentally process all the information you've gathered from your participants, it's important to keep a cool head. Yes, you should listen to prospective end users. But, be reflective. Consumers sometimes need guidance, and slavishly following their wants and desires can land you in real trouble.

One of my favorite episodes of *The Simpsons* (called "Oh, Brother, Where Art Thou?") nicely illustrates this point. Grandpa confesses that Homer has a half-brother, whom Homer immediately tries to track down. He eventually discovers that his brother is Herbert Powell, the head of a car manufacturer. Herb then decides that Homer, being an average American, is the perfect person to design a new car for his company. He gives Homer free rein in the design, and, as you might expect, Homer is determined to build the car with all sorts of wild effects, like bubble domes, tail fins, and several horns that play "La Cucaracha." At the unveiling of the new car, Herb is horrified to find that, besides being hideous, the car costs $82,000. Herb's company declares bankruptcy.

This raises an important question: When do you go with what your customers tell you, and when do you overrule them? Unfortunately, there's no simple answer.

In his best-selling book *Blink*, Malcolm Gladwell talks about how chair manufacturer Herman Miller developed the Aeron, and the dilemma the company faced when trying to measure people's reactions to new ideas: "It is hard for us to explain our feelings about unfamiliar things," Gladwell writes. The Aeron chair was a deliberate attempt by Herman Miller to design something different; the most ergonomically correct chair ever. As Gladwell points out, "In Herman Miller's years of working with consumers on seating, they had found when it comes to choosing office chairs, most people automatically gravitated to the chair with the most presumed status—something senatorial or throne-like, with thick cushions and a high, imposing back." (Sounds a lot like one of the clichés we discussed in Chapter 1, doesn't it?) "What was the Aeron?" Gladwell continues, "It was the exact opposite: a slender, transparent concoction of black plastic and odd protuberances and mesh that looked like the exoskeleton of a giant prehistoric insect."[4]

Sounds a lot like a disruptive hypothesis, doesn't it? Here are some of the responses Herman Miller got from testing:

- It looks like it came from the set of *Robocop.*

- The wiry frame will not have the strength to hold a person.

- It resembles lawn furniture.[5]

As Herman Miller discovered with the Aeron chair, we often react badly to things we aren't familiar with.

Consumers had a clear mental model of what an office chair should look like, something throne-like with thick cushions and a high imposing back. They were unsure what to make of this "exoskeleton of a giant prehistoric insect." It was comfortable, but ugly. "And if there was one thing that Herman Miller knew from years and years in the business, it is that people don't buy chairs they think are ugly." We often react badly to things we don't understand or that we aren't familiar with. But, as just mentioned, that doesn't always mean that the idea is without merit.

I'm sure you already know the rest of the story; you may even be sitting in it. Herman Miller didn't kill the project or cover the chair with padding. The company's decision makers trusted their instincts, and the Aeron chair went on to become one of the biggest product successes of the last decade. What was once ugly has become beautiful, and Gladwell finishes this thought by suggesting that "the problem with market research is that often it is simply too blunt an instrument to pick up the distinction between the bad and the merely different."[6]

The important thing in this process is to realize that new offerings (from the evolutionary to the revolutionary) take time for consumers/users to understand and get used to. So, you need to listen and observe their reactions, but be sure to listen and observe in the right way. Facilitating end user feedback in the way I've just described helps you create a distinction between quality and difference.

Which Idea Should You Use?
(Introducing Mr. Potato Head)

In the previous step, you had real live prospective customers help you refine your ideas. They compared, contrasted, told you what they liked, and what they didn't like. Now, it's the moment of truth: Which idea are you going ahead with? Well, as I hinted at earlier, the one you pick may not necessarily be the "winner" from the user testing. In fact, it's more than likely that you'll end up combining attributes from all three. That's the "Mr. Potato Head" part of the process. You start with your basic potato, add various features, and tinker until you're completely satisfied. Don't like the eyes? Take them off and put on sunglasses. Don't like the bald head? Add a hat. Think he'd look better with his nose on top of his head instead of in the front? Give it a try.

It's pretty much the same with your disruptive ideas. You start off with your basic potato, get rid of some of the things that don't work, and add a few from other potatoes that do a better job until you're able to clearly communicate your message. To help you through this process, we're going to create several prototypes—rough mock-ups of your selected idea; this is not a perfect, complete rendition of your product or service. Creating these prototypes allows you to better visualize, understand, and transform your disruptive idea into (finally!) a solution.

The results of prototyping—and its close relative, simulating—are all around us: movies, airplanes, automobiles, microprocessors, personal computers, software, gene sequencing, biotechnology, and even the Internet. But, as Michael Schrage writes in his book *Serious Play*, "The value of prototypes resides less in the models themselves than in the interactions—conversations, arguments, collaborations—they invite."[7]

Prototypes create a "shared space" for senders and receivers to communicate. As Schrage says, "Creating a dialogue between people and prototypes is more important than creating a dialogue between people alone."[8] Why? Because it's easier for people to express what they desire by reacting to prototypes than by verbalizing their needs. (This is absolutely critical. I couldn't possibly count the number of clients—and designers—who thought they wanted a particular button in a particular place, or swore up and down that some feature or other was vital. But after they had a chance to hold a prototype in their hand, they changed their minds completely.)

Prototypes make thinking tangible. They give shape to your ideas. Literally.

Prototypes make thinking tangible. They give shape to your ideas. Literally. They help highlight the context in which something will be used, uncover flaws in your assumptions, and help identify what's being left out (or what should be). But, perhaps their most important function is to force you to face up to the practical compromises that you'll inevitably have to make to deliver value to your market. In other words, it may turn out that your wonderful vision can't actually—and practically—be turned into a reality.

Be Quick and Dirty

The prototypes that I produce for my clients—and that I want you to produce—are supposed to be rough. I know it's tempting to try to create something really beautiful. But, I can tell you that the rougher the prototype, the more likely people are to get involved and work on it—and that's exactly what you want. The more refined it looks, the less people want to tinker with it.

The difference between the touchable and untouchable is what we, in design, call "fidelity." Low fidelity is cheap, easily changed, and can be thrown away without anyone worrying too much about it. Low-fidelity prototypes tend to encourage participation and dialog. High fidelity is expensive, well made, and much closer to the actual look and feel of a product or service. But you'll find, as many others have, that as the prototyping materials and the look and feel tighten up, so does a lot of the thinking.

You've probably noticed that I've been referring to prototypes—plural. That right there is one of the differences between design-oriented companies and non-design-oriented ones. In design, we always create multiple prototypes of the same idea. That helps us refine and change things around until we get it right. Non-designers tend to try to create and perfect only one.

It's important to keep in mind that we're operating in a time-limited context. That means that your prototypes should be "satisfactory" as opposed to "optimal." Big difference. Here's a good example:

> On April 11, 1970, the Apollo 13 Mission to the moon launched. Fifty-six hours into the flight, an electrical failure in the command module

required the three-person crew to retreat to the lunar lander. The carbon dioxide filters of the lunar lander were engineered to support two people for two days, which was the planned duration of the lunar landing. But to get everyone safely back to earth, they would have to support three people for four days. The square carbon dioxide filters of the forsaken command module had the capability to filter the excess carbon dioxide, but they wouldn't fit into the round filter receptacle of the lander.

On the ground, NASA engineers figured out how to construct a makeshift adaptor for the square command module filters (in other words, how to plug a square peg in a round hole). With time quickly running out, ground control instructed the astronauts on how to put together the adapted filters, using materials available on the spacecraft such as duct tape, covers from logbooks, and plastic bags. The makeshift adaptor wasn't perfect, but it solved the urgent problem of carbon dioxide poisoning. Had the engineers insisted on creating a perfect solution, they would never have finished in time.[9]

The bottom line is that, at this stage, prototypes beyond the satisfactory yield diminishing returns.

Iteration Cycles

Any idea can be expressed in a variety of ways. For example, if your idea is for a cup, you'll have to consider size, material, color, weight, location of the handle, whether or not it has a lid, and so on. You'll be developing your prototypes through a series of three design iterations, which will progress from low fidelity to slightly higher fidelity as you refine the idea and learn more about how it will be used.

In the context of design, the word *iteration* refers to the process of exploring variations of the prototype, continually shaping and tuning the idea. At the end of each cycle, the prototype is reviewed with other people and "iterated" in the next cycle based on feedback. Each cycle of iteration narrows the range of possibilities until the idea takes the shape of a feasible solution.

Set Up a Review Team

Never review the results of an iteration cycle by yourself. At a minimum, you should have one other person help you. More is definitely better. Other people will bring different perspectives and will see things in your prototypes that you can't or don't. They'll probe you for details that you forgot or thought were irrelevant.

So, who are these other people? You'll get the best results when your review team includes a broad range of perspectives. Ideally, include members of the target audience in one or more of the iterations to verify design requirements. Also, include stakeholders who will build or sell the idea. Their perspectives could be extremely valuable. If you think that I'm being a little vague, you're right. Normally, I try to be as specific as possible, but at this stage, every company's disruptive ideas, circumstances, finances, and philosophy are so different that there's no way to come up with a precise breakdown of the "other people" that will work for everyone—or anyone.

*Never review the results of an iteration cycle
by yourself.*

I recommend small group sessions of no more than 3–5 people. If your team is larger than that, you can run several sessions in parallel, where participants can work in teams of two or three. Review sessions are typically scheduled as small group sessions and last for 90–120 minutes. This allows a few minutes for a brief explanation of the prototype and still leaves plenty of time to play freely with it.

Recording Information

As you and your review team are working with and evaluating your prototypes, you should be collecting as much data from as many sources as you possibly can. On Post-Its, write interesting snippets of conversations, observations, comments, problems, obstacles, opportunities, strengths, weaknesses, faults and defects, cultural influences, questions, insightful quotes, and anything else that could possibly help with the next round of iterations.

What's Your Disruptive Solution? (Three Rounds of Prototyping)

Low-fidelity prototypes often consist of any of the following: paper, wire-flows (which are web-page mock-ups), foam-ware, clay, 3D printing (also known as "soaps"), and Velcro modeling, as well as click-through simulations and scenarios. Because your goal is to elicit the largest amount of useable feedback for the least investment in time and money, the materials you use will vary according to the situation you're in. That said, let me walk you through a three-round process that uses three different prototyping methods: one for the service and information components of your disruptive idea, one for the product component, and one that pulls all the pieces together.

Round 1: The Storyboard. Grab Some Paper.

When most people hear the word "prototype," they imagine that it's referring to a physical thing. But, as Michael Schrage writes, "A prototype isn't merely a prop on the organizational stage; it is a character in a marketplace narrative."[10] So in Round 1, I want you to think about your prototype as a character in a big-budget movie.

Looking at it that way, the fundamental question isn't, "What kind of prototype should I be building?" The reality is that the story is about the interactions end users will have with your disruptive idea. Or, as we at frog design like to say, "You aren't designing a product or a service. You're designing an experience." So, the question you should ask is, "What kind of interactions do I want to create?"

At this point, another perfectly reasonable question might pop into your mind: "How can I possibly make a physical mock-up of an experience?" The answer is that you're going to create a storyboard—just like the ones you may have heard about in the film business. But, instead of frame-by-frame drawings of important scenes, you'll be sketching step-by-step pictures of how people will accomplish specific tasks when interacting with your new offering. Storyboarding ensures that you won't overlook any intentions you might have or steps that might be critical to the end users' experience.

In one of my classes at NYU, several teams of students were working on creating new taxicab experiences. Storyboards were the perfect way to get their ideas across. They had drawings of what would happen when the customer first entered the cab, what was going on inside the cab during the ride, and what the customer's experience was at the end.

Think of a storyboard as a kind of comic book strip consisting of both pictures and words. But don't worry about your drawing skill or lack thereof. Stick figures, speech bubbles, arrows, and the like are all you need to get your message across. Simply draw a separate picture for each action the consumer takes while experiencing the key aspects of your idea. Add words to explain what's happening and include close-ups of details where needed.[11]

A prototype is a character in a storyboard narrative.

Round 2: The Mock-Up. Grab Some Velcro and Cardboard.

In this round, you'll create a three-dimensional "mock-up" of the overall structure for your product, as well as suggestions for functionality, use, and integration with your service and information components. This is a quick and inexpensive exercise that serves as an effective way of gaining additional input from your review team and learning how various elements of the product or task relate to one another.

This sounds like a product-centric approach—where do we put the buttons on our remote? But, even if you're creating a service, chances are you'll need some props. If you think about it, there are tangible elements to almost any service. And, in many cases, for the experience to work at all, you'll need some tangible elements. In the taxi experience, for example, one team wanted to incorporate a rating system so that riders could increase their chances of getting a good driver (safe and knowledgeable, for example). They came up with—and mocked up—a new rooftop light that displayed the driver's rating in stars, kind of like an Amazon.com or C-Net review. Another team wanted to create a taxi service for parents and children who need car seats. One of the things they had to mock up was a new kind of seat that swiveled around so that parents sitting in the front of the cab could easily turn around and interact with their kids. At the least, creating 3D prototypes gave them a chance to have a prop to demonstrate while explaining the new service to others.

To prepare, make a trip to the craft and/or hardware store to gather inspiration or use everyday household items. The exact materials you'll need will depend on the project, but here are some basics that should be in every prototype kit:

- Foam or plastic shapes: cones, balls, and cylinders in a variety of sizes

- Velcro, glue, felt, and duct tape

- Stickers: large, small, round, rectangular, colored

- Buttons, knobs, switches, caps, hinges

Generally speaking, the bigger the variety of materials you have available, the less constrained you'll be in creating and modifying your prototype. After you establish a basic features list, make sure there are a variety of items available that could fulfill that function. For example, you don't necessarily need real, live buttons or switches from a hardware store. You could use stickers, construction paper, tape, or simple illustrations instead.

You can construct your mock-up anyplace where there's a table that's big enough to spread out and build on. You may find it helpful to keep a stash of materials in small plastic bins or boxes so you can move your model-making workshop around anywhere you need to.

Round 3: The Video and/or Photo Scenario. Grab Your Camera.

As much as I love doing things on paper, there are some limitations. Perhaps the most important is that, with a paper prototype, it's difficult to show how you intend for something to be used. Sure, you can tell people about it; but if your idea is truly disruptive, people may need guidance on how to implement whatever it is that you're offering.

In this round, you'll produce a series of photos—or video scenes—of someone actually going through the entire experience in the actual environment. You may have a paper, wire, and foam mock-up of a taxicab swivel chair for parents, but in this round, you'll show a parent in a cab actually turning around to wipe some drool from a baby's chin. If you designed a new system that allows you to control every electronic device in your home, you'll show someone coming home and using the keypad to turn on the lights, preheat the oven, and start downloading her email. You might also show someone sitting in an office, taking care of the same tasks remotely via cell phone, or receiving a text message alerting the user that the burglar alarm went off. And, if you've designed a new web-based business, you'd show people navigating the pages, finding the information they need, placing orders, and so on.

The bottom line is that video (or, to a lesser extent, still photographs) can help people better imagine and envision how one could best leverage your idea by showing it in use and in context.

One last thing: You won't be entering your video prototype in the Sundance film festival. You're not going for award-winning performances, snappy dialog, or innovative camera techniques. This is a quick-and-dirty reel that you can shoot on any device and in any format—just as long as you have some rudimentary editing capabilities.[12]

Think Outside the Socks!
The Disruptive Solution

Before they went into production with any of these ideas, Jonah and his partners wanted to get feedback from their target audience and the retail buyers they would have to sell to. First, they needed to test the names they were considering for the company. So, armed with sheet of paper with different possible character names they had generated—like Miss Matched, Mismatched, Little Miss Matched, and so on—Jonah hit the streets of San Francisco and asked random tweens to tell him what they thought of each name. The winner, hands down, was Little Miss Matched, which was, in a sense, a triple entendre: A young miss who's all about matching, a young girl who's mismatched, and the fact that all of us feel a little mismatched now and then. The biggest clue that he was on the right track with Little Miss Matched was that everyone who saw that name smiled. It was a truly emotional response, not an intellectual one.

The watercolor paintings of sock patterns were great—and actually helped the company secure a small amount of seed money. But, to fully refine their idea into a market-ready solution, they had to produce some prototypes—actual socks that people could see, feel, and understand. The three partners were able to line up a meeting with the hosiery buyer for the entire Nordstrom chain. They presented their prototypes and, just a few minutes into the meeting, the buyer announced that the idea was "terrible" and asked why they thought she would possibly be interested.

Fortunately, the Little Miss Matched partners were clearheaded enough to ask the buyer—who'd mentioned that she had an 8-year old daughter—to take some of the samples home and get the girl's opinion. Two days later, the buyer called back with an order for $250,000 and brand placement in all Nordstrom stores.

Although I've been using *Little Miss Matched* as an example of how to implement the steps I'm outlining in this book, they also managed to fall into several of the traps I mentioned. For example, being design-minded, they wanted to create some unique packaging to display their first orders. So, they came up with something truly superb, innovative, dramatic... and completely impractical. The designers failed to anticipate how aggressively customers handle merchandise in the retail stores. The packages looked great but they wouldn't stay closed, leaving piles of Little Miss Matched socks all over the floor.

Taking Action
(What Do People Really Think?)

Use the following sample agenda to facilitate discussion, guide your thinking, and assist participants in improving on the ideas:

- Introduction (15 minutes).
- Who you are.
- Today's agenda.
- What your goals are.
- Go through the five steps:

  1. **Memory mapping** (15 minutes): Ask participants to draw, from memory, the product or service they currently use. What are their

thoughts and feelings about the situation at hand?

2. **Individual ranking** (15 minutes): Guide participants through each idea, allowing them to ask clarifying questions while reviewing the idea visualizations. Ask participants to rate the ideas' attributes on a 1–5 scale.

3. **Group ranking** (15 minutes): Participants use a worksheet that lists attributes and their polar opposites. You give them color-coded dots that represent each idea and have them work as a team to order the ideas relative to each other.

4. **Improvement exercise** (15 minutes): Participants work collaboratively to mix-and-match attributes and features from the ideas they have been shown to create one idea that the group agrees to be ideal.

5. **Open discussion** (15 minutes): Talk directly about what they value.

Taking Action (What's Your Disruptive Solution?)

Use the following **three rounds of prototyping** to shape your ideas into a single disruptive solution:

Round 1: Storyboard

1. Choose where to begin your story.

2. Select a sequence of interactions that communicate how a user experiences your idea.

3. Collect information from your research that will help craft the story: observations, insights, and so on.

4. Create the storyboard frames with pictures and words. Put only one action step within each frame.

5. Review with the team and record feedback.

Round 2: Mock-Up

1. **Preparation:** Consider a number of basic or possible forms that a product could take, and cut these forms out of a block of cardboard or foam core. Cover the forms with Velcro. Next, get a collection of objects that can serve as widgets (buttons, knobs, dials, and so on), and attach the other side of the Velcro to them. Now, you can configure the idea in a variety of possible representations. Feel free to use basic foam or plastic models (soaps), along with stickers, markers, or images.

2. **Build and iterate:** As you work your way through various iterations of the product being mocked-up, document why you're making changes. This is important because, at some point, you may want to go back to a previous version.

Round 3: Video

- Using your storyboard and initial mock-ups, create a video showing how a person interacts with your solution with enough clarity to be understood by others.

- Use a video camera or a point-and-shoot camera with video capabilities.

- Use iMovie or Windows Movie Maker for the video editing.

- Keep it simple and quick.

At this stage of the process, you've tested your ideas with prospective end users, selected a direction to refine, and prototyped it into a single, disruptive solution. To take that solution to the next level, you'll have to make a disruptive pitch that will persuade internal and/or external stakeholders to invest in or adopt what you've created. That's the focus of Chapter 5.

CHAPTER 5

Making a Disruptive Pitch:

Underprepare the Obvious, Overprepare the Unusual

"I opened the script and it exploded like a grenade into my face, and I closed it again because I was scared. He puts these crafty little devices in there that take you away from the security of your clichéd thinking."
—Christoph Waltz, Actor[1] (Describing Quentin Tarantino's script for the movie *Inglourious Basterds*)

Well, you're almost there. You started with some hypotheses, put them into context and defined an opportunity, generated several terrific ideas, and molded them into a single solution. Now, you've got a bit of a sales job on your hands. No, I'm not talking about selling to customers. Long before you get to that point, you'll need to sell your disruptive solution to the people within your organization or external stakeholders who control the purse strings.

Your audience for this pitch could be the budget people you have to convince to take the solution to the next level. Or the VC guys who want to evaluate your idea before they ask for a robust business plan. Or your R&D and marketing departments, so they can do more in-depth testing and analysis. Basically, you need general buy-in from anyone and everyone who might allocate the capital, manufacturing capacity, technology, and personnel to get your solution out of the conference room where you've been playing with prototypes and into the marketplace.

Most people don't adopt a disruptive solution because it's disruptive. They embrace it because they believe in the value it delivers. And you're going to need a lot more than a basic presentation to earn that confidence. You have to help them feel their way toward disruptive change, step by step. And that change needs to be easy to adopt, motivating, and clear in the value it provides.

I'm going to tell you right now that the pitch I'm talking about isn't going to be an easy task. You may have the best solution in the world, but if you don't come up with a persuasive story of why it matters, it's not going anywhere. Oh, and did I mention that you've got about 10 seconds to grab your audience's attention and another 8 minutes and 50 seconds to keep it until they tune you out and start tweeting or updating their Facebook status?

I know that 9 minutes doesn't sound like much, but if you need more than that to tell your story, you haven't thought it through well enough and you'll lose your audience. Having done hundreds of these presentations—and listened to thousands more—I can guarantee you that it won't get better as it gets longer. Quite the opposite. (On the other hand, you don't want to go too much shorter than 9 minutes. If you do, you're in danger of slipping into "elevator pitch" mode, and that's a place you definitely don't want to be. I'll talk more about that later.)

You've got 10 seconds to grab your audience's attention and another 8 minutes and 50 seconds to keep it.

Think about a movie preview. If the producers really want to get you excited about seeing a movie, they know they have to hook you quickly with the title and the narration by that guy with the great voice ("In a galaxy far, far away, where everyone's trying to sell something, it takes a truly disruptive idea to stand out. And only one person can create it..."). After that, they have less than 5 minutes to persuade you with the rest of the trailer. Previews rarely last longer than that.

Author W. Somerset Maugham once said, "There are only three rules for writing a novel. Unfortunately, nobody knows what they are."[2] To paraphrase Maugham, there are only three rules for presenting the results of disruptive thinking. Fortunately, we know exactly what they are: A good, 9-minute pitch starts by creating empathy ("Why should I care?"), continues by building tension ("I'm curious to see where this is going"), and finishes by turning your audience into believers ("Hey, this is great. How do we implement it?").

Nine Minutes to Pitch

Why am I suggesting that you keep your pitch to 9 minutes? Because it promotes precision. There's a wonderful example of this principle in the movie *Without Limits*, which chronicled the friendship between running star Steve Prefontaine and his coach Bill Bowerman, who co-founded Nike, Inc. We see everyone on the running team—except the coach—assembled for a meeting in the bleachers of their school stadium. Prefontaine impatiently asks his teammates, "Why does Bowerman call a team meeting for 7:58? What's wrong with 8:00?" At that moment, Bowerman arrives, "Hold on. I'll tell him why, gentlemen," he says. "7:58 promotes the question: 'Why 7:58?' And everybody gets here at 7:58 to find out why."

Giving you a 9-minute time limit forces you to be precise in your thinking and organization. That, in turn, will help you pack as much meaning into those minutes as you can. Your being precise also makes your audience pay more attention to what you have to say. And the more attention they pay, the more firmly the information you have to share will be encoded and retained in their brains.

Another reason for keeping your pitch short is that your big moment may happen completely unexpectedly. Keeping the pitch to a manageable 9 minutes ensures that you'll always remember the important details.

That said, do not confuse your 9-minute presentation with an "elevator pitch." They aren't the same. Not even close. Over the years, I've come to hate that term—and I'm not alone. In her book *Good in a Room*, former Hollywood executive Stephanie Palmer writes, "The problem is that the term 'elevator pitch' is misleading. While it does capture the importance of clear, quick, effective communication, it also encourages us to make three classic mistakes: Pitching in the wrong places (e.g., elevators); pitching to the wrong people (e.g., people in elevators); pitching the wrong things (e.g., cookie-cutter concepts)."[3]

Stephanie should know. As part of MGM's executive team for six years, she was pitched elevator-style almost everywhere she went: by a receptionist at her dentist's office while she was clutching her jaw in pain, by a cabbie on a 5-minute ride to her hotel, by a real-estate agent at an open house, and even by a yoga teacher before class. None of these pitches were ever developed.

Quick Note on Structure

Although I've spent a lot of time talking about how important it is to upend clichés, in this chapter, I rely on one of the biggest clichés of all: the PowerPoint presentation. Frankly, I'm not a big fan of PowerPoint, but because so many people know exactly what it is, we're going to break your 9-minute presentation into nine slides, 1 minute each. As you put your slides together, remember to keep them as visually appealing as possible. Photos, graphics, video, and a few bullet points. But, don't let yourself fall into the trap of filling the slides with text and then reading them. Zzzzzz.

You'll divide your pitch into three 3-minute sections—one for creating empathy, one for building tension, one for making them believers—plus some unspecified time at either end for introductions and discussion.[4] Unspecified is not a synonym for "unlimited," but you do have a little less control over those sections. So, for now, let's focus on those all-important 9 minutes.

Please Hold Your Questions

Ideally, you want to fully immerse your audience in what I like to call a "flow state"[5] for your entire presentation—a state where they're so absorbed in whatever you're saying that they stop thinking about the worries and frustrations that they brought into the meeting (or anything else, for that matter, including what's for lunch and where the bathroom is). If you succeed, your audience will have experienced a modified sense of time. What was 9 minutes on the clock will seem like 3, you'll have piqued their curiosity, and they'll be motivated to further explore your solution.

So, throughout those 9 minutes, keep your audience focused and free from distraction. That means that, before you even start your presentation, lay down the law: no phone calls or texting, no wandering in and out, and please hold your questions and comments until the end. If you don't do this, you risk losing control of your audience (along with any hope of getting them into a flow state) before you even make your opening remarks. I've seen it a million times.

I know this may sound harsh, but hopefully, you're dealing with a group of adults who should be able to play nicely and focus for 9 whole minutes.

What Happens if You Have a Larger Block of Time to Make Your Pitch?

As I've pointed out, making your pitch longer isn't going to make it better. So, consider using the extra time for an extended post-pitch discussion, and if need be, a more relaxed introduction sequence. Having more time to get your audience engaged at these bookends is a worthy use of extra time.

A longer presentation time also may be useful if you have more than one solution to present, which is often the case in business. If so, you should still follow the three-stage sequence for each solution. Why? Because you can't expect to gain your audience's attention just once at the start and have them hanging on your every word for 30, 45, or 60 minutes. The 9-minute tune-out phenomenon will still happen, and you'll have to hook them all over again by creating more empathy and building more tension.

Nine Minutes to Pitch.

Building Empathy: Your Introduction and the First Three Slides

Let's get back to our 9-minute presentation—actually, to just the first few seconds of it. It turns out that what happens during those opening moments greatly influences what listeners will learn and, more importantly, what they'll remember. As the author of *Brain Rules*, John Medina puts it, "If you're trying to get information across to someone, your ability to create a compelling introduction may be the most important single factor in the later success of your message."[6]

In my experience, for a compelling introduction to work, you must get the audience emotionally involved: They must feel empathy. So, how do you introduce emotion in the opening 3 minutes?

The best way is to quickly establish the inadequacy of the status quo and then use one relevant, real-world observation from your research to bring a point of frustration to life for your audience. You want them to believe how dysfunctional the status quo is and feel like they are experiencing the pain for themselves.

Of course, most people completely waste their first 3 minutes—the most important ones in the presentation—by going broad instead of deep. They give a general overview, free of any telling details: "First we did this, then we looked at that, then we plotted the information on this framework, then we noticed that blah blah, and then we went back and looked at this again…." Or worse, they spend these opening minutes reviewing an agenda of what they're going to talk about. (The first stage of the traditional "Tell 'em what you're going to tell 'em. Tell 'em. Then tell 'em what you told 'em" approach that has been putting audiences to sleep for decades.) Although that may be solid advice for preparing a book report in grade school, it's completely inappropriate for disruptive pitch situations. Presentations that open that way lack empathy. Any emotion required from the audience dissolves, and they feel nothing.

One of the best-known examples of avoiding this trap and doing it right is the tale of London advertising agency Allen Brady & Marsh's pitch to British Rail in 1977. The details of the story change depending on who's telling it or what point they're trying to illustrate, but it usually goes something like this:

> The client team arrived at the agency at the appointed time, to be greeted by an uninterested receptionist who took a break from filing her nails for just long enough to direct them towards a small sitting area where the seats were stained, ashtrays were overflowing, and the tables were littered with coffee cup stains. She didn't even bother to offer them anything to drink. The clients waited, and waited, and waited. As the scheduled time for the agency's presentation disappeared into the past, they asked the receptionist what was going on, and she tersely replied that someone would "be along in a minute." Their frustration grew, until at the moment they were about to pick up their bags and leave, Peter Marsh, the agency head, appeared before them. "Gentlemen," he said. "You have just experienced what hundreds of thousands of people experience every day on British Rail. And we'd like to talk to you about how to put that right."[7]

Now, that's a bit lengthy for the first 3 minutes of a 9-minute pitch, but you get the idea. Peter Marsh gave the clients a visceral and emotional feeling for how bad things are in the current situation. The status quo has a firm hold on most people's perceptions, so you need to shake them out of a complacent perspective.

The best way to shake them is through some well-placed sensory details—the more senses you can involve, the better. In the British Railway example, the clients were put in a position where they were emotionally neglected by the receptionist and the head of the ad agency, visually (and probably olfactorally) assaulted by the shabby surroundings and overflowing ashtrays, and generally disrespected by being kept waiting for a ridiculously long time.

If you can figure out a way to involve your audience emotionally, terrific. And if you can combine *two* senses—specifically touch and sight—you'll greatly increase the chances that you'll make a lasting connection. In 3 minutes, you won't have time to talk about every single thing you uncovered in your research observations. But that's okay, because you only need a few tidbits that are rich in sensory detail—the audience's imagination will supply the rest. As the legendary film director Orson Welles once said, "...give the audience a hint of a scene. No more than that. Give them too much and they won't contribute anything themselves. Give them just a suggestion and you get them working with you."[8]

Make a list of the attributes of the research observation you're describing. Cross off everything that seems generic, and from what remains, select three or four key details that are unique to the situation at hand. If you can bring one or more of these details to life with a physical prop, even better. Here's how to structure your first three slides.

Slide 1: The Status Quo

To set the scene, you need to quickly and effectively demonstrate a problem of parity in your industry, segment, or category situation. Look back through your competitive audit and the clichés you uncovered. Use those clichés to demonstrate that everyone is doing the same thing, competing the same way, or that nothing has changed in a long time.

Example: If the company is Starbucks, the fact that baristas are serving cappuccinos everywhere now, even at McDonald's and 7-Elevens, should be a parity problem. (But of course, on this slide, the example you'll be using is your own situation.)

Slide 2: The Observations

Put the focus on the consumers. Look back through your research observations around tension points, and choose three or four to highlight in your pitch. Remember, the more visual and sensory-rich your observations, the better your audience will remember them. You can do this by using photographs and/or video footage, combined with a great quote from one of the consumers you spoke with earlier in the process. But, be careful. If the pictures and words don't tell the same story, you'll be inhibiting the audience's ability to recall them.

Slide 3: The Story

For people to take action on your solution at the end of the pitch, they have to feel empathy at the beginning. And the way to make them care is through the details of one key story from your research activities. What did you hear or see that could bring the points of frustration to life for your audience in the most memorable way?

In the British Railway example, the story was that customers are emotionally neglected, visually assaulted by the shabby surroundings, and generally disrespected by being kept waiting by ridiculously long delays.

Building Tension: Slides 4–6

In this part of the pitch, you'll explain the opportunity you see, and your insights about it, in a way that, hopefully, elicits surprise, interest, and curiosity.

In his book *This Means This, This Means That*, Sean Hall asks readers to vote on which of two sentences is the best. "The cat sat on the mat.," or "The cat sat on the dog's mat?"[9] I know that may sound painfully simple, but it illustrates the point beautifully. If the cat sat on the mat, does anyone really care? Cats sit on mats all the time. But, if the cat decided to curl up on the dog's mat, well, that's a different thing. There's a good chance that if the dog finds out, he'll have a serious problem with someone messing with his mat. Was the cat trying to provoke the dog? How did the dog react? Is the cat still alive? Again, it's a simple example, but it shows how effective some tension can be.

Tension is at the heart of every compelling story, which makes it rather surprising that it's usually glaringly absent from most pitch presentations. Most of the ones I've dozed—I mean sat—through have been some variation of "Boy meets girl and lives happily ever after" (product meets consumer need and sells happily ever after). Not emotional and not believable. If you're going to pique an audience's interest, you need a major piece of tension that throws the status quo off kilter. In other words, "Boy meets girl. Boy loses girl.

Boy wins girl back." In disruptive pitch terms, "Boy meets girl" is all about empathy. "Boy loses girl" is tension. "Boy wins girl back" is where the audience truly believes.

Tension is what gives a presentation the zing it needs to be meaningful and memorable. To set up the emotional component of your presentation, you first need to introduce your audience to a counterintuitive insight and opportunity.

Slide 4: Tell Them What They Don't Know (The Insight)
A presentation without tension is usually a presentation built solely on common sense, on information the audience already intuitively knows. (The prevalence of common-sense presentations is what probably gave rise to the rather sarcastic definition of a consultant: someone who takes your watch and then tells you what time it is.)

What's wrong with appealing to what the audience already knows? Plenty. When people hear something they already know, they tend to tune out. And if there's one thing you don't want during your presentation, it's an audience that has mentally left the room. Your pitch has to be something your audience will remember long after you finish your presentation. And the way to make that happen is to create some tension between what they already know and what you want them to know.

Interestingly, the definition of "common sense" can change, depending on the audience. I've often found, for example, that what's common sense for the consumer is often uncommon sense for the producer. While working on a project for office printers, we noticed a disconnect between the ways manufacturers and consumers load paper into their machines.

Manufacturers generally design their printer trays to hold a full ream of paper—500 sheets. Seems a lot easier to just rip the sheath off, place the whole thing into the tray, and shut the door. Good, old-fashioned common sense, right?

But, our observations of consumers in their office environments revealed a different story. It turns out that people never put a full ream into the tray. For them, it was just plain common sense that the printer would jam if they put in the full ream (the fact that this wasn't true didn't seem to matter). So, they'd rip open the package and put only about 350 pages into the printer. I'm sure if you've ever been anywhere near an office printer, you've seen numerous partially used packages of paper.

The point is, what's obvious to one group of people may not be at all obvious to another. To the right audience, even the most mundane details can come as a revelation. It's all about creating a disturbance, a disruption, between what your audience assumes they'll get and what you actually give them. Common-sense, tension-free presentations do the opposite: They give the audience exactly what they were expecting. And that's the kiss of death.

In putting together slide 4, use the following steps as a guide:

- Review the key insight that gave rise to your opportunity.

- Frame the insight in such a way that it breaks your audience's expectations. That means emphasizing the part that is uncommon sense—the part they don't know or aren't expecting. For example, don't just tell them that people think cars are important for transportation (common sense). Emphasize the finding that owners rarely describe their vehicle as a mode of transportation. Instead, they use words like protection, rescue, and office (uncommon sense).

Slide 5: Give Them a Turning Point (The Opportunity)
In Hollywood terms, the result from this kind of unexpected tension is a turning point. That's the plot twist that takes the story in a new direction and makes the audience ask themselves, "How is this thing going to turn out?"

Master screenwriter Robert McKee says that turning points have to surprise, increase curiosity, and present a new direction. If the turning point is compelling enough, it'll keep the audience in their seats until the closing credits roll. In the movie *Jaws*, for example, the audience wonders, "Will the sheriff kill the shark, or the shark the sheriff?"[10]

So, how do you introduce a turning point? The good news is that you've already got everything you need. Remember the disruptive opportunity from Chapter 2—that key insight and supporting opportunity—which you built your disruptive ideas and solution around? That's what you're going to use to create the turning point for the pitch. A disruptive opportunity is to a pitch what a turning point is to a movie.

In Chapter 2, I used the example of an opportunity to satisfy an unmet need in automobile design by optimizing productivity features for drivers who aren't actually driving. The automotive industry places such a high value on the driver's and passenger's experience while the car is moving, that an opportunity focused on the experience of using a car when not driving came as a surprise, piqued their curiosity, and presented a new direction. This was a turning point.

Pitching the insight and opportunity should provoke your audience to wonder what, exactly, your solution will be. So, finding the turning point means looking back through your research findings to pull out the key insight and opportunity that inform your solution. After that, your job is to communicate them to your audience—in a counterintuitive way that wreaks havoc with their expectations. Then, back up your claims with plenty of supporting logic.

For the printer project mentioned earlier, the turning point was framed around a price-point insight. We discovered that one of the biggest indicators of quality—at least in the minds of consumers—is the upfront price. If a printer costs between $300 and $600, buyers tend to worry about the machine's robustness. If it's under $300, they immediately dismiss it as simply "not meant for the office." The problem was that the inkjet printers we were researching were in fact, built for office use. But, compared to the bulkier, more expensive laser printers, people saw inkjet printers perceived as cheap toys for home use. In this context, "home use" was a disastrous association.

The conventional strategy for selling inkjet printers is "razor and blades"—that is, sell the printers for next to nothing and make your money from expensive refill cartridges. The turning point was a complete retraction of this strategy. In other words, we were going to try to make money on the "razor" too; in this case, the printer. This opened up the opportunity to build features into inkjet printers and raise the price until it was roughly the same as a comparably outfitted laser printer. We supported this assertion with evidence that, in general, people didn't do long-term burn analysis on the difference between ink and laser cartridges. In other words, they focus on the purchase price, not the total cost of ownership. So, the plan was to keep the price of the cartridges the same, but double the price of the printer so people would see it as competing head-to-head with the more expensive lasers. Can you imagine being told that the only way you'll be taken seriously is if you double the price of your product? That's a turning point with a smile.

To sum it up: Review the opportunity area that gave rise to your solution (Chapter 2). Once you have the opportunity described, add credible logic with key supporting observations, and facts gathered from your research. For example, the observation that, "people rarely describe their vehicle as a mode of transportation" supports an opportunity to provide "productivity features" for drivers who aren't actually driving (a turning point for in-car experience). Sometimes, it's more powerful to illustrate your point with photographs or clearly stated quotes from your research. For the printer project, we showed numerous photos of the consumers we observed and their quotes that supported the price-point opportunity we were describing.

Slide 6: Make It Familiar (The Analogy)

A minute or so ago, you'd grabbed your audience's attention and piqued their curiosity by introducing your counter-intuitive opportunity as the turning point. Now that you've surprised them, things have dramatically changed. You no longer need to spark their curiosity. Instead, you need to spark their understanding. The sooner your audience truly gets what your opportunity is about, the better. That means that the potential of the opportunity has to be intuitive.

I know, I know—after all the emphasis on turning points, breaking expectations, and being counter-intuitive, why would I suddenly go for something as mundane as "intuitive?" Because when an audience encounters a new opportunity, they tend to respond by comparing it to everything they've learned when they've been in similar situations and confronted with similar issues. They can't help themselves—it's just something people naturally do. It's much easier than consciously trying to learn something new. And you haven't got time for an extended course in thinking outside the box.

Given all that, you need to tilt the playing field in your favor by controlling the associations they make. This gives you a far better chance of getting the reaction that you want rather than leaving it to chance. In other words, to make your solution resonate, you need to quickly signal to your audience that it is disruptive, yet familiar. And the easiest way to do this is to juxtapose it with an example of something they're already familiar with.

This form of juxtaposition is sometimes called "high concept," and the movie business is full of these descriptions. For example:

- *Speed* is *Die Hard* on a bus.

- *13 Going on 30* is *Big* for girls.

- *Alien* is *Jaws* on a spaceship.[11]

"The compact, five-word phrase '*Die Hard* on a bus' pours a breathtaking amount of meaning into the previously nonexistent movie of *Speed*," write Dan and Chip Heath in *Made to Stick*. "...[T]hink of all the important decisions you could make, just on the strength of those five words. Do you hire an action director or an Indie director? Action. Do you budget $10 million for the movie or $100 million? $100 million. Big star or ensemble cast? Big star. Target a summer release or a Christmas release? Summer."[12]

With the printer project, the solution was to offset consumer bias against inkjet printers by leveraging the positive associations they had with laser printers. In other words, we could build into inkjet printers some of the things consumers liked about laser printers. To make the point, a high-concept analogy from the automotive industry was used. Volvo has reinvigorated station wagons by borrowing tough attributes from SUVs and incorporating them into their XC70 station wagons. They have successfully reengaged the station wagon owners who were at risk of defecting to SUVs.

As you see from this example, the important thing when using a high-concept analogy is that the analogy must come from a different and non-related industry. If you're using an analogy from the same industry that you're focused on, it's not really an analogy—it's a me-too copy—which defeats the purpose of disruptive thinking.

To make the analogy memorable, take inspiration from those movie examples and boil it down into a short, compact phrase—your equivalent to *"Die Hard on a bus."* Little Miss Matched did this effectively to communicate their vision with the statement, "We're doing for socks what Starbucks did for coffee."

Ready to try one on your own? Fill in the blanks in the following statements, juxtaposing the meaning of your opportunity with an analogous example (such as another brand, product, or service that your audience will recognize) from a non-related industry. Generate a few alternatives for each and then refine the one you think best compares your disruptive thinking to something your audience already knows.

This is _____ (analogous example) for _____ (your category).

Example: This is the Volvo XC70 for inkjet printers.

Or

We're doing for _____ (your category) what _____ (analogous example) did for _____ (alternative category).

Example: We're doing for socks what Nike did for running shoes.

Making Your Audience Believe: The Final Three Slides

Your audience's reward for having paid attention for 6 whole minutes (which, hopefully, has seemed only like 1 minute) is that they now get an overview of the solution you've created. You want to quickly build their belief in your solution by concisely describing what it is and how it works; the advantages for customers and stakeholders of making the changes you're suggesting; and finally, why your solution is meaningful in a broader context.

Slide 7: The Solution

To get things rolling, start by presenting the solution's name, a brief description, a visual of how it works, and the key points of difference that separate it from other offerings in the market. We covered all of these components in Chapter 3, when you came up your disruptive idea—so you probably have some of this content already started. However, your solution may have evolved since the original idea was created, so now is the time to go back and refine those steps as necessary.

Speaking of key points of difference, I said in the Introduction that you want to be considered the *only ones* who do what you do. But if the phrase, "We don't have any competition," flashed through your mind, it's important that you make a serious effort to banish that thought for the presentation. There is no quicker way to kill a disruptive pitch than to claim you're all alone on Mount Everest and that no one can catch you. To prospective investors, competition is often seen as a good sign. It lends a little weight to your proposal by demonstrating that there's an issue that someone else besides you thinks is worth addressing.

Look back on the competitive audit you did in the disruptive hypothesis stage (Chapter 1), and pull together a list of potential competitors from that industry, as well as any others that may be relevant. Hopefully, in the disruptive idea stage (Chapter 3), you already thought about some of the differences between your idea and what else is out there. Now, it's time to make those differences obvious to your audience. In our inkjet printer project, we did this by declaring that we were "playing laser's game better than laser," and listed the key reasons why.

Every solution has four basic components: a name, a one-sentence description, a visual, and the key points of difference. All four components should appear together on one slide.

The name should accurately represent the solution and make it stand out. It should be short, memorable, and credible. You may already have a name for this solution, one that you developed in the idea stage (Chapter 3). If so, review the name and change or refine as necessary.

Identify the core value of the solution and the key benefit you need to communicate. Then, craft a brief description that captures the essence in one sentence. Again, you may already have a description from the idea stage (Chapter 3). If so, review it and change or refine as necessary. If not, follow the steps laid out in Chapter 3.

You need to be able to visualize your solution to concretely describe its components, features, and functionality. Change, refine, or increase the fidelity of the visual you started in the idea stage. If key components of the solution have changed since then, create a new visual.

You haven't got time to go into a bunch of minor differences. You probably identified some key points in Chapter 3. If not, look for and emphasize one or two really big differences.

Slide 8: Make Change Appealing (The Advantages)
After you make it clear what you want to change (empathy) and why (tension), you need to persuade your audience that the changes deliver clear advantages to the people who will use and implement the

solution. You need to shift the focus of your audience from the *need* for disruptive change to the *motivation* for disruptive change.

Shift the focus of your audience from the *need* for disruptive change to the *motivation* for disruptive change.

To communicate advantages, you should think about who would be eager to initially have and use your solution. The answer lies in the "early adopters."[13]

Generally speaking, all commercial offerings progress sequentially through four stages: introduction, growth, maturity, and decline. Your focus right now is on the introduction, the official birth of your disruptive solution. Focusing on the introduction stage means that you'll need to work closely with early adopters to refine and tune your solution before it gets anywhere near a mainstream market.

Why? Because, for a disruptive solution to really take off, you must introduce it to people who have the motivation to appreciate the change in status quo.

These people like being part of disruptive change, and if you succeed, they'll tell the next group, which will pass the word on to the mass market. In demonstrating why the creators of Napster initially targeted college students, Seth Godin wrote, "They combined the three things necessary for the virus to catch on: fast connection, spare time, and an obsession with new music."[14]

Keep in mind that early markets are small, so don't focus your pitch on convincing your audience of how huge a potential market is. Only mainstream markets are huge, and disruptive solutions never get their start in mainstream markets. Promising that is a sure-fire way to lose credibility with your audience. So, think small and target only early adopters where you can make an impact with what Gary Hamel calls, "revolutionary goals, but evolutionary steps...."[15]

After you consider the advantages for the early adopters, turn your attention to articulating the motivation for the key stakeholders involved. Pay particular attention to anyone whose help you'll need to implement the new solution.

Your list of stakeholders should be as broad as possible and will include account suppliers, partners, and alliances—not just the decision makers in the room. If you want to get any stakeholders to shift to your disruptive solution from something else, you'll need to show them the advantages of doing so, and you'll have to convince them that the change is worthwhile.

- **Suppliers:** What will motivate key suppliers? How does your solution benefit potential suppliers? Are they integral to the success of the solution? Is there value in business goals being more closely aligned?

- **Partners:** Consider what will motivate critical partners in the development of your solution. What partners do you need for this solution to work? How could these partners be motivated in a creative way?

- **Alliances:** Is a joint venture or strategic alliance with another company required? Is there another company that could be motivated to share the risk and rewards involved in your solution? Is there a mixture of resources that could be advantageous for this solution?

Slide 9: Leave Them on a High (The Ethos)

An ethos gives your solution a higher purpose, something that goes beyond pure functional and emotional value. It's the narrative theme around which people will remember your solution. Whenever I talk to clients about creating an ethos, Nike is one of the first brands that pops into their minds. That's no big surprise—after all, Nike's tag line, "Just Do It!" may be the most recognized slogan in the world. But, the real reason it's so memorable is that it represents more than just a product. "If one had to put the matter succinctly, it was that 'Just Do It' was not about sneakers," said Scott Bedbury, one of the Senior VPs of Nike responsible for the campaign, "It was about a brand ethos."[16] That ethos represented a call to action for ordinary athletes that meant get off the couch and jog; be active at something you enjoy.

An ethos also opens the door to more expansion across multiple categories than the traditional notion of a single-product value proposition. What you're doing here is giving people a feel for how big the solution could get, how far it could expand. Little Miss Matched did this nicely in its brand book, coming right out and saying, "I'm the first voice in history to say, 'Mix it up!' Today I'm socks; tomorrow I'll be... bikinis and flip-flops for summer. Tights, gloves, and scarves for winter. Pj's and slippers for bedtime (and a whole lot more)." I'm not asking you to create a polished, public-facing tagline here. What I am suggesting is that you come up with a concise and profound phrase that sums up your solution's message to the world. What's it saying? What's it challenging? What's it provoking? By declaring that, "Taking a trip is more than just going for a drive," frog designs' automotive client captured the idea that the in-car experience had little to do with driving.

Think Outside the Socks!
The Disruptive Pitch

As we discussed in Chapter 5, if you want to stimulate interest in your new product or service, your disruptive solution requires a disruptive pitch. In the case of Little Miss Matched, this meant thinking beyond a standard PowerPoint presentation. To this day, when Jonah pitches their story, he relies on a much lower-tech option: a handmade "brand book." The book is essentially a tangible business plan that helps articulate exactly what's so unique and disruptive about Little Miss Matched.

On page 1, we see an image of Little Miss Matched herself, smirk and all. "Hi," she says. "I'm Little Miss Matched." On page 2, she boldly declares, "I'm the first voice in history to say that nothing matches but anything goes." On page 3, she announces that, "I'm doing with socks what Starbucks did for coffee and Nike did for shoes." Over the next few pages, Little Miss M talks about her socks and other products that the company plans to expand into, including bedding, swimwear, hats, gloves, and even television shows and movies.

The brand book is just part of the pitch. Little Miss Matched also sends out a "box of fun," filled with sock samples and a hand-written note inviting the recipient (they send these only to CEOs) to talk about their disruptive solution. It's a remarkably successful formula and has allowed them to tell their story to the CEOs of FAO Schwartz, Linens 'n Things, JC Penney, Foot Locker, Toys R Us, and many other stores that have ordered millions of dollars' worth of mismatched socks. In late 2008, Little Miss Matched did a large deal with Macy's and closed a $17 million funding with the same investment partners that backed *Build a Bear*. With 6 retail stores and over 150 employees, Jonah and his partners are a long way from where they started 5 years earlier.

Taking Action:
9 Slides in 9 Minutes

Use the following list to create a 9-minute pitch **for your solution** that takes your audience from their pre-presentation, "Why should I care about this?" **(empathy)**, through the mid-presentation, "I'm curious to see where this is going" **(tension)**, to a post-presentation, "Hey, this is great! How do we implement it?" **(belief)**.

Creating Empathy (3 Slides, 3 Minutes)

Slide 1: The Status Quo
Slide 2: The Observations
Slide 3: The Story

This is the point of orientation for your audience, where your objective is to spark their empathy. Establish the inadequacy of current clichés (The Status Quo); explain why this is an issue (The Observations); and how that's frustrating the target customer (The Story).

Building Tension (3 Slides, 3 Minutes)

Slide 4: The Insight
Slide 5: The Opportunity
Slide 6: The Analogy

This is the point of surprise, intrigue, and curiosity for your audience. Your objective is to build tension by introducing something they don't know (The Insight). Then, provide a sense of how this knowledge could be used (The Opportunity), and a familiar example to help them understand the potential (The Analogy).

Making Them Believe (3 Slides, 3 Minutes)

Slide 7: The Solution
Slide 8: The Advantages
Slide 9: The Ethos

This is the audience's reward for having paid attention, because now they get an overview of your solution. Your objective is to build their belief by introducing the answer to the opportunity (The Solution); the motivation for customers and stakeholders to make the change you're suggesting (The Advantages); and the solution's higher purpose and possibility (The Ethos).

Quick Reference Guide

Process Summary

My aim in writing this book is essentially to convince you that the attitude, "If it ain't broke, don't fix it" is the enemy of disruptive thinking. It's more effective to start by identifying something in your business that's not necessarily a problem, in a place where others wouldn't expect to look. In other words, think about what usually gets ignored, pay attention to what's not obvious, and start with things that ain't broke. Then go about methodically breaking them down by following the steps I laid out.

This guide is intended as a fast, practical reference point for those steps. It outlines 3 questions for each stage of the Disrupt process, and the actions required for the answers.

Crafting a Disruptive Hypothesis

Objective: To generate three deliberately unreasonable "what if" questions that will enable you to break through the boundaries of your category, segment, or industry situation.

What Do You Want to Disrupt?

1. Define the high-level situation in the industry, market, or category you want to disrupt (for example, a situation in which nothing has changed in a long time).

- Resist the urge to start thinking of problems. The best hypotheses are often created from situations where nothing appears to be wrong.

- Fill in the blanks: "How can we disrupt the competitive landscape of [insert your situation] by delivering an unexpected solution?"

What Are the Clichés?

2. Identify the *clichés*—the assumptions and conventions that influence the way producers and consumers think about the situation you've selected.

   - Start by comparing two or more companies that are competing in the industry you're focused on.

   - Using the three filters (product, interaction, and price), scour the Web for information about each competitor and make a list of the clichés you find. (Remember: The most obvious and seemingly "natural" assumptions are the easiest to ignore.)

What Are Your Hypotheses?

3. Take the clichés and twist them like a Rubik's cube, subjecting them to fresh scrutiny. (Remember: This exercise is designed to challenge your established way of looking at an industry, segment, or category.)

   - Examine the clichés and look for something (or things) that you could take away, invert, and exaggerate in scale.

   - Generate several hypotheses by asking, "What if...?"

- Choose three hypotheses that you're excited to move forward with.

Discovering a Disruptive Opportunity

Objective: To find an opportunity to put your hypotheses into action, by carefully observing your customers and their needs.

What Are Your Observations?

4. Determine the kinds of information you'd like to gather by making a list of questions based on your hypotheses.

5. Define the relevant audience: a mix of the target customer population, potential customers, and/or outlier customers.

6. Work out the timing required. Your decision will depend on the size and complexity of your focus, but it should be a rapid immersion—2–3 hours for a quick informal study, 2–3 days for a longer one.

7. Set up interviews and observations in the environment where people use the products and services relevant to your situation.

8. Allow for multiple observation sites so you'll be able to collect rich information across several environments.

9. Do at least two of the following:

   - Open-ended interview and observation

   - Noninvasive observation

   - Intercept

10. Look for tension points, not pain points (nagging issues that linger for a long time without receiving much attention). These include Workarounds, Values, Inertia, and Shoulds versus Wants.

- Make sure that you document everything you're doing in at least two ways—notes and photographs.

What Are Your Insights?

11. Ground your data by printing or transcribing your observations. Print key photographs, sketches, or other images you collect.

12. Find a surface that's large enough for you to move and arrange all of your observations and supporting information.

13. Cluster related observations together and identify key themes, and then seek to turn observations into insights.

- Look for the non-obvious, the unexpected. Look for a counterintuitive rift between expectation and result.

- Generate insights by asking "why?" Interpret the patterns you see, and record your insights in real time. Aim for one insight per theme.

- Give your insights impact. Use paradoxical phrasing (but or whereas) to call attention to the gap exposed by the insight.

What Are Your Opportunities?

14. Match your insights with the relevant hypotheses to determine the best fit.

    • Consider the relationship between insights and hypotheses. Look for the advantages that your insights suggest.

    • Group and re-group. Combine the insights with the hypotheses in different ways to find the best opportunity.

15. Define one opportunity that provides the most fertile ground for putting your hypotheses into action. (Remember that an opportunity is not a solution. It defines a focus area for the creation of solutions.)

    • Describe the opportunity in a three-part sentence (who it's for + the advantage it delivers + the gap it reveals).

Generating a Disruptive Idea

Objective: To transform the opportunity into three ideas with the potential for great impact.

What Is Your Focus?

16. Break down your opportunity into a number of focus points for generating ideas (e.g. Opportunity: Provide drivers with ways of being *more productive* that are *safe and optimized* for driving).

    • Note the *advantage* part of the opportunity statement (e.g. More productive), then list 4–5 moments for *when* this benefit could be delivered (e.g. When making phone calls in the car).

- Note the *gap* part of the opportunity statement (e.g. Safe and optimized for driving),
  then think about *how* this could be addressed
  for each of the *when* moments (e.g. How can
  we safely optimize the way people make
  phone calls in their car?).

17. Think creatively about the answers to each ques-
    tion, and generate as many new ideas as you can
    (e.g. Idea: Integrated hands-free phone calls).

    - For inspiration, look for examples of how
      that *advantage* or *gap* has been addressed in
      other product or service categories.

    - Figure out how you could connect the entire
      idea or part of the idea into your situation.

What Can You Blend Together?

18. Pick three ideas that offer the greatest differ-
    entiation and the largest number of benefits to
    either your customers or your company. (Choos-
    ing three gives you a good range to experiment,
    challenge assumptions, and gather feedback in
    the next stage.)

19. For each of the three ideas, go through the follow-
    ing steps to refine the offering:

    - **Blend the bits:** Consider the product, ser-
      vice, and information bits simultaneously to
      create a hybrid offering.

    - **Blend the benefits:** Consider the benefits
      being offered to partners, buyers, and users.

What Are Your Ideas? (Describe them.)

20. Follow these steps to create a one-page summary for each of your three ideas:

    - Give your idea a name. Make it short and memorable.

    - By using four components (Label, User, Benefit, and Method), craft a one-sentence description of what the idea is and why it's important.

    - Describe how your idea is different. Include one significant point and several minor ones.

    - Visualize. Create an annotated visual for your idea that concretely describes its components, features, and functionality.

Shaping a Disruptive Solution

Objective: To facilitate end-user feedback and use it to refine your ideas into a single, feasible solution.

What Do People Really Think?

21. Recruit consumers for research.

22. Bring them into your office (or wherever you'll be doing the testing), and run them through the following five activities:

    - **Memory mapping:** Ask participants to draw (from memory) the product or service they currently use and that's most relevant to your situation.

    - **Individual ranking:** Guide participants through each idea and ask them to individually rate the ideas' attributes on a 1–5 scale.

- **Group ranking:** Have participants work together to rank the ideas against a list of attributes and their polar opposites.

- **Improvement exercise:** Have participants work together to mix and match attributes and features from the ideas they have been shown. By doing this, they agree on the one idea that seems ideal.

Which Idea Should You Move Forward With?

23. Based on consumer feedback, select one idea to refine.

   - Alternatively, combine attributes from all three ideas by getting rid of some things and adding a few from other ideas that do a better job.

24. Set up a review team of 3–5 people that includes a range of job functions and perspectives.

   - Include members of the target audience and stakeholders who will build or sell the idea.

25. Prepare to create rough mock-ups of the idea that will enable you to visualize, understand, and transform your idea into a practical solution.

What Is Your Solution?

26. Complete three rounds of prototyping to refine and shape your chosen idea into a feasible solution:

   - **Round 1:** Create a storyboard that illustrates the interactions end users will have with your solution. Highlight the service and information components of the idea.

- **Round 2:** Create a physical mock-up (low-fidelity), highlighting the product component of your solution.

- **Round 3:** Produce a series of photos—or video scenes—of someone using your solution in its proposed environment (context). This will convey how the product, service, and information pieces work together to form a cohesive experience.

27. As you and your review team are working with and evaluating the prototypes, collect as much feedback as you can.

   - At the end of each cycle, review the prototype with other people and "iterate" it in the next cycle based on feedback.

   - Each cycle of iteration narrows the range of possibilities until the idea takes the shape of a practical solution.

Making a Disruptive Pitch

Objective: To craft and deliver a 9-minute pitch for your one solution.

How Are You Creating Empathy?
(3 Slides, 3 Minutes)

28. This is the point of orientation for the pitch audience, where your objective is to spark their *empathy*

   - **Slide 1:** Establish the inadequacy of current clichés (The Status Quo).

   - **Slide 2:** Explain why this is an issue (The Observations).

- **Slide 3:** Explain how that's frustrating the target customer (The Story).

How Are You Building Tension?
(3 Slides, 3 Minutes)

29. This is the point of surprise, intrigue, and curiosity for the pitch audience. Your objective is to build *tension* by delivering an unexpected insight and opportunity.

   - **Slide 4:** Tell them something they don't know (The Insight).

   - **Slide 5:** Provide a sense of how this knowledge could be used (The Opportunity).

   - **Slide 6:** Use a familiar example to help them understand the potential (The Analogy).

How Will You Make Your Audience Believe?
(3 Slides, 3 Minutes)

30. This is where you unveil your solution to the pitch audience. Your objective is to build their *belief* in the value it delivers.

   - **Slide 7:** Reveal your answer to the opportunity (The Solution).

   - **Slide 8:** Explain the motivation for customers and stakeholders to make the change you're suggesting (The Advantages).

   - **Slide 9:** Communicate the solution's higher purpose and potential (The Ethos).

PART III

The Disruptive Leader

CHAPTER 6

The Disruptive Leader's Motivation:

A Different Attitude

"We have a good ability to see what's possible and not
be impeded by the status quo."
—Larry Page, CEO, Google[1]

Are you an innovator? Have you been told to think differently because it's better to lead change rather than react to it? Is it your job to lead change as if being new and improved is an end in itself? Do you feel pressured to Google and Tweet the latest inventions in "Tech," or listen to TED talks, hoping to get inspired by other people's stories of shattering the status quo? Or maybe your job is to help sell someone else's creativity so that millionaires who want to become billionaires can rake in the profits, leaving you with not nearly enough for your efforts. Sounds ridiculous, doesn't it? Well, enough of the relentless pursuit of the next big thing. Don't you think it's time to disrupt the disrupters?[2]

Innovation for Growth:
Better Recipes

I don't take it for granted that you're motivated to *disrupt*. In fact, if anything in the preceding paragraph rings true, I suspect you might sometimes lapse into an attitude of "innovation fatigue," worn out by endless talk about the need to change whatever you're doing and replace it with something else entirely. I do, however, take it for granted that you're motivated to *grow*. But, whether you realize it, the two—innovation and growth—are connected: If you're motivated to grow, you also have to be motivated to lead innovation because this is not another transient management fad. It's what drives economic growth. If you don't innovate, you can't grow.

A few doors down from my office at NYU Stern School of Business sits professor Paul Romer, the economist who, in the early 1990s, challenged the conventional wisdom about how we think about growth. "To create valuable final products, we mix inexpensive ingredients together according to a recipe," Romer writes, "...growth springs from better recipes, not just from more cooking."[3]

For the previous hundred plus years, theories of economic growth were based on the idea that growth could be explained only by increases or decreases in labor, land, or capital, and that resources in the material world were finite. Think of the California Gold Rush. The first nuggets discovered in 1848 led 300,000 gold-seekers to invade the then-sleepy town of San Francisco, and by 1850, most of the gold had been collected. Growth that couldn't be explained by an increase in labor, land, or capital (that is, new ideas) was seen as an element of chance. Things such as climate, geography, and government determined the pace of innovation, and it was nearly impossible to do anything about them. Some economies were just more fortunate in these areas than others.

In his published research, *New Growth Theory*, Romer pointed out that there's a big difference between the world of tangible *things* and the world of intangible *ideas*. When we share "things," we make them less valuable. (You don't pay as much for a used car because it has already been used.) But ideas don't work like that—they're an inexhaustible resource with no inherent scarcity. In other words, although the world of tangible things is subject to diminishing returns, the world of intangible ideas is not.[4]

Take, for example, this ballpoint pen I'm writing with. My use of this pen prevents someone else from writing with it at the same time. It's an exhaustible resource—something tangible that's subject to decreasing value and diminishing returns. One pen is worth a lot to me right now as I sit alone writing, but what if someone were to offer me a second pen? I might be able to use it if it had different color ink, but it's not as valuable to me as the first one. If someone else were to offer me a third pen and a fourth, what use are they? There's not much extra value (when writing alone) in having two pens, let alone three or four.

But now imagine that the ballpoint pen is an *idea*. You can't give away your pen and still write with it, right? But you can give away the idea of the pen and still keep the whole thing. No matter how many times you tell somebody how to make or use a ballpoint pen, that idea isn't diminished or worn out. Instead, the opposite happens—the consumption of the idea is subject to *increasing returns*. The more ideas you generate, the more you can generate; disseminating useful ideas tends to spark more useful ideas. The more popular the idea, the more valuable it becomes. Innovation is an item of investment—ideas become products and generate wealth. It's the opposite of a gold rush, where as more treasure hunters flocked to California in 1849 looking for gold, the faster that gold ran out.

Growth occurs whenever people take ingredients (resources) and rearrange them into recipes (ideas) that make them more valuable.

Growth occurs whenever people take ingredients (resources) and rearrange them into recipes (ideas) that make them more valuable. A recipe for a ballpoint pen might look something like this: A writing instrument that features a tip that is automatically refreshed with ink. It consists of a precisely formed metal ball seated in a socket below a reservoir of ink. As the pen is moved along a writing surface, ink is delivered.

Now that one hundred million ballpoint pens are sold every year and seem to be readily available everywhere, we take them for granted. But it took almost 60 years for someone to rearrange the ingredients of a fountain pen so that the tip didn't need to be constantly dipped in ink. (Of course, there are also recipes for the ink, the assembly of the parts, the packaging, the labeling, and the shipping.)

Cooking up ingredients in a kitchen is a useful metaphor for disruptive thinking and leadership.[5] Every organization has ingredients such as competencies, assets, and processes that together form a recipe for a new way of offering something to the market. Have you noticed how many reality cooking shows there are on prime-time television? (Think "Master Chef," "Cutthroat Kitchen," and "Chopped.") They typically take place in a warehouse that includes a large kitchen area with several cooking stations. Thousands of amateur and professional chefs around the country audition for a chance to show off their culinary chops through a series of time pressure tests and team challenges under the direction of the master chefs.

Now imagine these cooks surrounded by shelves full of new ingredients, ingredients that unfortunately won't get used because they don't fit into traditional recipes. What a wasted opportunity. It's similar with traditional thinking and leadership. Executives use the same old recipes over and over again to repeat their success and avoid mistakes, uncertainty, and the wastefulness of trial and error. New ingredients (potentially disruptive new technologies and insights into consumer behavior) often go unused because they don't fit existing products, services, and business models.

It's not easy to break free of the "we've-always-done-it-this-way" approach. But if you truly want to find new recipes, that's what you'll have to do, because the problems with innovation often have less to do with the ingredients themselves than the way we put them together. Simply rethinking or rearranging your ingredients often leads to profound new recipes and shifts in perspective. Coca-Cola, for example, began as a pharmaceutical product. Tiffany & Co. started as a stationary store. Nokia began as a paper mill. Avon, the cosmetics company, started out in door-to-door book sales.

In a widely cited example,[6] Wendell Weeks, the CEO of Corning, told Steve Jobs that Corning had developed a chemical exchange process in the 1960s that led to what it named "Gorilla Glass." Jobs told him he needed a major shipment in six months, despite the fact that Corning wasn't making it and didn't have the manufacturing capacity. But an immediate rethink of its Harrodsburg, Kentucky, facility led to a full-time change from making LCD displays to Gorilla Glass for smartphones and tablets. As a result, Gorilla Glass is now a $1 billion-a-year business for Corning.

Don't feel that you have to wait for new technology before you can create new recipes for innovation. The truth is that you can create a new recipe anytime you see that the current one is running on autopilot. To do that, you'll either have to focus on ingredients that you're currently overlooking (they won't be particularly hard to find when you realize that there's a 1:1 ratio between the amount of thinking attention resources receive and their contribution to profit) or rethink the ingredients themselves.

Consider one of Nike's most successful new products in recent years—the Flyknit Racer—which required a complete rethink of the traditional manufacturing process. (It's not surprising that Nike calls its R&D center the Innovation Kitchen.) The traditional shoe recipe involves cutting rolls of pre-woven material into pieces and then stitching and assembling them. But with Flyknit, a shoe's upper and tongue can be knitted from polyester yarns and cables, removing the need for multiple layers of fabric. Nike uses only as much thread as it needs in production, and the shoe can be tightened here and stretched there to improve fit. The result is a shoe that's not only more environmentally friendly, but can also reduce long-term production costs. Flyknit isn't a new recipe for a shoe—it's a new recipe for the manufacturing process. Nike's Innovation Kitchen rearranged the ingredients to get more value out of what was already available by disrupting the sewing machine. "One of my fears is being this big, slow, constipated, bureaucratic company that's happy with its success," says Nike CEO Mark Parker. "Companies fall apart when their model is so successful that it stifles thinking that chal lenges it."[7]

Innovation Capital:
Ideas as Currency

As Nike's CEO observes, the danger for companies is becoming overly cautious. They're thinking and doing what everyone else is thinking and doing, all the while hoping to do it little more cheaply, faster, or better. If everything has to work this quarter, then by definition, you don't have time to pursue risky, disruptive ideas. Actually it's not the ideas themselves that are risky; the only thing being risked is the time it would take to get those ideas to a point where they're worth experimenting with further.[8] The more thinking time you're willing to risk, the less you'll risk other resources.

New Growth Theory helps us understand that an idea is itself an item of investment. Every idea gives an organization another way of thinking about its business, another choice. Think of ideas as currency—a source of *innovation capital*. The more ideas you have in your portfolio, the more capital you have available to "purchase" other ideas.

Every idea gives an organization another way of thinking about its business, another choice.

So instead of grasping at Option A as the single, right direction, innovation capital positions your business to do Option A, B, C, or D—or any combination of those choices—depending on the circumstances. The greater the uncertainty around those circumstances, the more options you'll need in the future. Your chance of creating new wealth is directly proportional to the amount of innovation capital you have available. Disruptive thinking and leadership is about putting your business in situations in which you have more new ideas to spend than your competition does.

Take Google, for example. A company best known as a search engine and advertising platform is relentlessly pursuing ideas that could reinvent its business and insure itself against catastrophic change that could render it obsolete. The breadth of its innovation capital[9] includes Calico, a research and development company working to extend the human lifespan;

driverless vehicles, which reached the 500,000 mile benchmark without an accident; Google Fiber, which is providing broadband Internet and cable television to a growing number of American cities; Shopping Express, an experiment in same-day delivery with national and local retailers; robots that can walk and run; Google Now, an intelligent personal assistant that proactively delivers to you information that it predicts you may want; and an electronic "throat tattoo" that can be a temporary microphone for a mobile device. There's also Google Ventures, a growth accelerator that keeps its innovation capital flowing by investing in more than one new company every week. "It's natural for people to want to work on things that they know aren't going to fail," says Google CEO Larry Page. "But incremental improvement is guaranteed to be obsolete over time.... So a big part of my job is to get people focused on things that are not just incremental."[10]

Many companies feel that it's a total waste of time to pour scarce management talent into speculative ideas. After all, the thinking goes, we're not Google. But you don't need the resources of a Google, Amazon. com, or Apple to boost your innovation capital. These days, it's easier, faster, and cheaper to test new recipes than ever before. Nearly all the resources you could possibly need to try something new (website, smartphone app, product prototype, service simulation, and business model scenario) are available as inexpensive, pay-as-you-go services or free, open-source software. You can get all your computing power and digital storage online, and all it takes is a couple of days to create a mockup or pilot. Ideas require more insight than money.

Of course, many new recipes will fail. Google, like any other organization, can't expect that every one of its ideas will turn into a blockbuster success; it can't possibly guarantee that the time (and money) it spends experimenting with an idea will be productive. More than half of all startups in American are out of business within five years, and three-quarters of startups backed by venture capital fail to recoup their investment.[11]

So the first thing we need to acknowledge is that most speculative ideas are going to fail. Even after rearranging your ingredients and taking the time and effort to consider each new iteration, you might find that they just aren't as useful as the traditional recipe you'd like to replace. But focusing too much on this small downside could make you completely miss a big upside. Constantly expecting success will invariably make your company risk-averse and will quickly eliminate a lot of interesting options.

Treating ideas as innovation capital is a commitment to a process, not to a result. The time-honored logic that dominates portfolio investing also applies to investing in ideas: Minimize the risk of the overall portfolio by diversifying your investments. With a diversified portfolio, encouraging people to experiment with a constant stream of disruptive ideas matters far more than actually adopting any single idea.

Bottom line: You need your people to be ready, willing, and eager to continually rearrange ingredients to find better recipes—regardless of the outcome. The real test isn't what or how much you know; it's what you do with your knowledge. You learn something from every new arrangement that you can apply to something else. (The simple idea of a wheel unleashed millions of new options for what to do with it.)

If you can capture what you learn and share it throughout your organization, you'll be helping your company increase the odds that the next idea you pursue will hit the target. As you continue to build innovation capital, releasing the energy that's been locked up doing things the way you always have and applying it to new ways of thinking, you'll eventually start seeing results. Experimenting with more options will ultimately force your business to think more clearly about trade-offs and better understand your priorities.

Innovation Capability:
Cult of Personality

The media fawns over celebrity tech CEOs such as Steve Jobs, Jeff Bezos, and Elon Musk, and regularly reminds us that they are (or should be) role models of innovation. Glossy magazines love reporting on their provocative antics, and business professors celebrate them as world changers.

A year after Steve Jobs died, Walter Isaacson's biography of him was still a best seller, and his life story had become a holy scripture for innovators, which prompted a cover article in *Wired* magazine to ask, "Do you really want to be like Steve Jobs?"[12] The article recounted a number of stories about Jobs' managerial cruelty and how he violated social or business norms to get what he wanted. (He routinely told subordinates that they never did anything right.) At the same time, it gave examples of how Jobs' brash personality helped him challenge several decades of conventional wisdom about the importance of worker empowerment and consensus decision making.

Fast Company magazine humorously described such tactics as "The art of talking trash"[13] and speculated that even though it's not taught in business schools, the ability to sling insults or shamelessly boast may explain how disruptive companies succeeded in an era consumed by niceness. Each of the CEOs it profiled—Box's Aaron Levie; Tesla's Elon Musk; William Morris Endeavor's Ari Emanuel—shares an ability to use provocation as the spark of innovation, both in their companies and in their industries. T-Mobile CEO John Legere, for example, opened a press conference by launching into an obscenity-filled critique of the wireless-industry practice of locking customers into pricey long-term contracts, which he called "the biggest crock of sh*t I've ever heard in my entire life."[14] Legere continued the assaults throughout the year by unveiling an "Un-carrier" strategy, and, dressed as Santa, he dropped lumps of coal into stockings embroidered with the logos of AT&T, Sprint, and Verizon. Anecdotes such as these suggest that in the ordinary course of business events, leaders of innovation tend to use their personality as much as their minds, insisting on their own point of view and shutting out other perspectives.

This brings up a very important point: When organizations get praised for their disruptive thinking, it's often assumed that charismatic CEOs are interested in innovation and can motivate everyone else in the rank and file. That may be true in some cases, but it's definitely not the rule. And the idea that you have to be a risk-taker to even think of an unusual idea or that you have to be an extrovert to inspire people to step outside their comfort zones is flat-out wrong.

The problem with the "cult-of-personality" approach to innovation is that, despite their charisma, too many leaders make no practical attempt to teach disruptive thinking as a leadership capability. And how could they? It's simply impossible to rely on skills you develop in the natural course of managing a business and leveraging its existing asset base, unless disrupting the business and *ignoring* the existing asset base is a requirement of the job. An obsessive focus on the C-suite no longer makes sense in a world dominated by flat organization structures where a small increase in disruptive thinking across every function and role in the organization could be more valuable than having a few innovative (and loud) people at the top.

Passive narratives of domain-specific leaders of innovation being provocative—no matter how subtle or acute—are not the same as active confidence and capabilities that work across functions and industries. Talking about innovation and actually *leading* it are very different things. And simply describing the *need* for disruptive thinking and leadership doesn't do much to help *achieve* it.

Disruptive leadership doesn't make sense in any reasonable, rational moment of management, but it's a skill that no reasonable, rational manager can afford to be without. It is not something you can outsource to an "innovation consulting" firm or delegate to R&D. Every leader in your organization—starting with you—needs to understand that it is part of their job description, that they need to do it regardless of any internal or external pressures, and that it's a core competence they need to develop regardless of their personal leadership style.

As the eclectic mixture of personalities on cooking reality shows demonstrates, with the right motivation, everyone can learn how to take raw ingredients that you'd never think could coexist in the same recipe and turn them into a delicious meal. In a similar way, learning the techniques of disruptive thinking and leadership are available to anyone who chooses to adopt them. This doesn't mean that everyone is going to be equally effective. But just as you can learn to follow a basic recipe to prepare food, you can develop confidence in your ability to motivate people to think disruptively and, more important, to lead the process. The more you practice, the more effective you can become.

Learning the techniques of disruptive thinking and leadership are available to anyone who chooses to adopt them.

Brash personalities make for good TV, but being a jerk won't magically make you a disruptive leader.

CHAPTER 7

The Disruptive Leader's Mindset:

A Different Awareness

> "Are people really going to do this?
> I would never do this."
> —Paul Graham, co-founder Y Combinator
> (Referring to Airbnb)[1]

If you're in a leadership position in an organization that sees no need for change, you don't have much motivation to break down ingredients (resources), rearrange them into new recipes (ideas), or create more value and wealth (growth). But if you want to succeed, you'll have to start doing exactly that. And it all starts with changing the way you think and learning to question *everything*.

Conceptual Innovation:
Self-Imposed Boundaries

Different organizations have different opinions about what kind of leadership behaviors will work best for them. However, most organizations have no idea that their future success will be governed by their *conceptual innovation* skills.

Did the phrase "conceptual innovation" make your eyes glaze over? If so, I get it. I actually hesitate to use the word "conceptual" because in many people's mind, "conceptual" is essentially a synonym for "talking (or thinking) things to death and not getting enough done." But "getting stuff done" usually means getting stuff done within the boundaries of what you believe is achievable and acceptable. Those boundaries—(think of them as "conceptual limitations") are imposed by your mindset—a way of thinking that leads you to evaluate and respond to new ideas in a certain way.

The most valuable (and largely untapped) resource that many companies have is the mindset of their employees, and the point of departure for driving innovation is the mindset of its leaders. Assumptions of what will or won't, what can or can't, what should or shouldn't be disrupted are all woven into your—and your employees'—mindset. And that mindset is what determines the freedom of your thinking and your organization's future.

Mindset is what determines your conceptual limitations, and, ultimately, the future success (or failure) of your organization.

Over the 20 years I've been involved in innovation, I've had the opportunity to teach a wide range of students in a wide range of settings. Whether it's tech CEOs in Silicon Valley, undergraduate students in China, United Nations delegates, grad students, or executive MBA students in New York, the one thing they have in common is that I can learn more about them from what they *don't* think about than from what they do. In my experience, most conceptual efforts are focused on continuity. In other words, people generally think about what they're thinking about for the sole purpose of supporting what they've already been thinking about. They spend time arguing over details and convince themselves that they're making decisions, when the truth is that they're neglecting important conceptual matters because those ideas don't lend themselves to concrete actions. (If you're not looking in the right direction, no amount of "taking action" will help you.)

"Ideas are the easy part," they claim. "The difficult part is the implementation. It's the execution that matters." That kind of thinking drives me crazy because what it comes down to is that they're not interested in ideas; they're interested only in *successful* ideas. They're willing to reap the benefit of those successful ideas, but anything short of that is more bother than it's worth. When leaders start challenging conformity and continuity (the "we've-always-done-it-this-way" philosophy) in organizations that are designed to enforce conformity and continuity, they're just creating work for themselves. In their mind, a new idea needs to be so straightforward that everyone immediately appreciates its value, because investing time in new ideas makes sense only if you succeed.

For the sake of discussion, I'll agree that an idea that's been developed and put into action is more valuable than one that hasn't. But what's even more important is the conceptual skill of being able to see value in ideas that *haven't* been developed. And that depends less on the idea itself and more on the mindset of the person who's judging it. If you believe that leaders who evangelize the need to disrupt their existing business are soliciting (and eager to accept) disruptive ideas, you're making a big—and potentially very costly—mistake. Whether they're aware of it or not, most executives, managers, entrepreneurs, and venture capitalists are biased toward evolution rather than revolution.

The problem is that the conceptual innovation skills that disruptive leaders need aren't always intuitive. In fact, it's counter-intuitive to search for alternative ways of thinking about the business when the business is at the peak of its success. It's counter-intuitive to slowly experiment with long-term solutions when you need to address short-term problems. We educate leaders to be reasonable, rational decision makers and then we expect them to be irrational, unreasonable "disruptors" hot on the trail of breakthrough innovations.

What it comes down to is that a leader's ability to challenge assumptions is more important than the ability to reinforce them. But if he or she has been trained to recognize only common problems and respond only with common solutions, the counter-intuitive mindset I'm talking about never develops. The disruptive leader's role is to help people (including themselves) get past their conceptual habits and biases. They need to foster disruptive thinking and ensure that all their employees know when and how to do it.

Keep in mind that this is a commitment to a conceptual *effort*, not to an applied result. You can't possibly keep people motivated if the only way you have of encouraging disruptive thinking is to implement every disruptive idea someone comes up with. By focusing on the process, you can encourage disruptive thinking and not feel bound to accept or act upon the products of the disruption. The unexpected questions those ideas raise are sometimes far more important than the predictable questions they were designed to answer. So having people willing to generate ideas that have never been considered before (even if they don't get used) is more important than having people routinely exercise restraint and sound judgment. The innovator's mindset is the most important driver of innovation.

The unexpected questions ideas raise are sometimes far more important than the predictable questions they were designed to answer.

Conceptual Continuity:
Holding the Horses

After the fall of France in the early days of the Second World War, weaponry of all types was in short supply. The British soldiers, faced with having to defend the coast, found themselves needing to use mobile cannons left over from the Boer War. The advantage of these cannons was that they could be hitched to trucks and moved around quickly if needed, but complex firing procedures made them slow to fire. In an effort to simplify the gun's operational procedures, the British command asked a time-motion expert to take some slow-motion pictures of the soldiers performing the loading, aiming, and firing routines. After studying the pictures again and again, paying careful attention to every detail of the routine, the expert noticed that in the moment before firing the cannon, two of the crew members did something strange: They ceased all activity and came to attention for a three-second interval while the cannon discharged. Confused, he showed the odd behavior to an experienced colonel of artillery. The colonel, too, was baffled. But when he looked at the pictures again, he realized what the problem was, "Ah," he said, "I've got it. They're holding the horses."[2]

The horses, of course, were long gone during World War II, but the old military practices and their accompanying mental models lingered on. The term *mental model* is a bit of technical jargon from psychology that describes a *conceptual continuity* of thought or behavior (see Chapter 4). Mental models are images or representations of assumptions and habits that you formed from your experience or borrowed from the experience of others. They're a convenient way of bringing together experience, feelings, and judgments that may be too vague or too complex to be verbalized.

Think about the mental image you have of a city you know well. Just as you can visually grasp the sentences you're reading as a pattern of recognizable words, you can identify districts, landmarks, roads, and pathways in that familiar city and see how they're grouped together in an overall pattern. You know where paths came from and where they lead. You get your bearings from the landmarks along those paths, which help tie the city together and give you a sense of direction. You use this image to move about easily and quickly, to find public transportation, a coffee shop, or the closest park. In other words you've developed a mental model of that city—a broad frame of reference to help you interpret the information you encounter, make decisions, and take action. All of your mental models work the same way. They're patterns of prerecorded information stored in your memory that narrow down the range of possible decisions and propel you forward on daily basis. They help you make educated guesses based on past experience, even if that past experience may not in your best interests today.

Consider the introduction of antilock brakes on automobiles.[3] Despite the measurable safety benefits in controlled tests with trained drivers, research indicates that antilock brakes haven't reduced the frequency or cost of accidents in real-world driving situations. The likely cause is that the mental model required to operate antilock brakes differs radically from the one many drivers use when they use conventional brakes. In fact, they're diametrically opposed (see the following table). Slamming the brakes on a wet, slick surface while steering away from trouble is exactly the *wrong* thing to do.

Mental Model for Conventional Brakes	Mental Model for ABS Brakes
On slick surfaces...	On slick surfaces...
Depress the brake pedal smoothly.	Depress the brake pedal fast and hard.
Pump brakes to prevent brakes from locking up.	Do not pump brakes.
Do not steer while braking, except to counter-steer.	Steer while braking.
Noise and vibration are signs that something is wrong.	Noise and vibration are signs that the system is operating properly.

Although mental models can be abstract generalizations such as "beware of strangers," or concrete procedures, such as how to use the brakes in my car, the most important point is that they shape our thinking, often in very profound ways.[4] If we assume strangers are dangerous, we think differently than we would if we assumed they were safe. If I assume that my car will stop when I pump the brakes on wet, slick surfaces, I'll continue to pump the brakes. We believe our assumptions are true, and our perception tends to support those assumptions. We notice and exaggerate behavior that reinforces our internal images and ignore whatever contradicts those images. In other words, we see exactly what we expect to see and that confirms and strengthens our view that we were right in first place.

Understanding the ways that mental models influence our thinking is vital to any company, because the most crucial mental models in any organization are those shared by key decision makers. Leaders individual thinking habits collectively shape the organization's habits.

Business decisions follow the direction that leaders set. Those same leaders then look for and find evidence that supports their decisions, which in turn accelerates the process of reinforcing the underlying mental models they used to make the original decisions. Their understanding of what business they're in and how they make money becomes dependent on a narrow set of preconceptions. The more successful a company and its management has been, the more rigid its habits.

The Engine Is Running

Most leaders are good at establishing mental models but not nearly as good at changing them or bringing them up to date. They never believe that their habits of thinking are in any way deficient because, being inside the system, they're blind to the problem. It's hard to imagine alternatives when you depend on a set of assumptions and habits, when that set of assumptions and habits serves you well, and when everyone around you has the same assumptions and habits. As the old saying goes, "It's difficult to get someone to understand something when their salary depends upon them not understanding it."[5] As a result, an organization's range of actions is generally limited to what is comfortable and conventional.

In the 1990s, Kodak and Fuji were slugging it out for dominance in the 35mm film industry. Meanwhile, digital photography had already begun to extinguish the market for analog film. At the height of its power, Kodak employed more than 140,000 people and was worth $28 billion. Ironically, it invented the first digital camera. But today, Kodak is trying to recover from its 2012 bankruptcy, and Instagram has become the face of digital photography.

Kodak wasn't the only company that got supplanted by Instagram. Remember Polaroid? It developed a chemical process that essentially mimicked a darkroom, but right in front of you in just a few seconds. In the 1960s and early 1970s, Polaroid employed 21,000 people and had a monopoly in the instant photography market. Its sales accounted for approximately 20% of the overall market for film and 15% of the U.S. market for cameras.[6]

If you think about it, Instagram is Polaroid photography in a different form—both were in the business of putting images into your hands right away. Unlike Kodak, Polaroid was well aware of the power of electronic imaging and was heavily involved in the field early. By 1989, Polaroid was spending 42% of its R&D budget on digital imaging, and by the late 1990s the company was a top seller of digital cameras. But they weren't able to take advantage of that early success. As digital cameras from other manufacturers started entering the market, Polaroid began losing some of its big customers in the real estate, insurance, and photo identification businesses. Film sales collapsed, and in October 2001, the company filed for bankruptcy.[7]

So why has Instagram been such a success while well-funded behemoths such as Kodak and Polaroid have failed? In large part, it's because Kodak's and Polaroid's top management couldn't (or wouldn't) change their mindset to respond to new market realities. They saw themselves primarily as being in the film business and assumed that customers would always want hard-copy prints. Their enormous profit margins reinforced those assumptions. So when sales began to decline, management was caught by surprise. As Polaroid's former CEO Gary DiCamillo recalled, "We knew we needed to change the fan belt, but we couldn't stop the engine. And the reason we couldn't stop the engine was that instant film was the core of the financial model of this company. It drove all the economics."[8]

Have you ever had a discussion with someone about Kodak or Polaroid? The next time you do, I'll bet you'll find a trace of the smugness that comes from knowing what *should* have happened. "Why couldn't they see the future of digital photography? It was so obvious! I mean, *I* could see it coming." This tendency to reconstruct the past to fit with present knowledge is called *hindsight bias* (or, more commonly, *20-20 hindsight*).[9] After something has happened—such as Kodak or Polaroid filing for bankruptcy—we look back and can clearly see what went wrong and why anyone with half a brain should have seen it coming.

Gary DiCamillo's analogy of the car mechanic captures the reason it's so hard for leaders to start thinking disruptively: How do you stick your hand into an engine that's running (your current business model) to change the fan belt (your current mental model)? Even if Polaroid or Kodak could have developed Instagram, they probably would have quashed it anyway. How would you respond to an idea that promised to save the company with an iPhone app that had no prospect for revenue? In both companies, leadership was under pressure to replace sales of instant film with something that was equally profitable and had gross margins in excess of 65 percent.

Here's one of the great ironies in business. When our mental models cause our business to fail, we know exactly what to do. We adjust them. But when our mental models make our business successful, we see no need to change them.

Conceptual Competencies:
The Curse of Best Practices

Mental models are often inherited in prepackaged form. In business, we call it *best practices*: borrowing a successful way of doing something from another company or industry. (If you've ever participated in a brainstorming session, you've seen first-hand how the concept of best practices keeps everyone in the room thinking the same way about a particular business or industry.)

At their core, best practices are no more than a proven way of allocating resources within the industry in which they operate. They're useful, but when you buy prepackaged best practices, you're buying into a zero-sum game: Putting things together in a certain way for one practice makes it difficult to put them together in a different way for a different practice. For much of the 20th century, the best practice many industries used was some variation of the "razor and blades" concept: If you hook your customers with a free or cheap product below cost (the razor handle), you can charge a lot more over time for the necessary add-ons to that product (the blades). The concept was set in stone, and a lot of leaders still accept it. "We make our money by making desktop computers as inexpensive as possible but getting users to spend big bucks on software licenses." Or "We make our money by selling our video game consoles for less than what they cost to manufacture, but we get $50 a piece for the games." The problem is that many companies become so fixated on maintaining today's best practices that they don't see that those practices are actually decaying. There's no rational reason to look for a better way of doing something if what you're already doing works just fine. And things get worse with time. The longer we hold a set of assumptions about what success looks like, the more value we attribute to those assumptions and the less likely we are to give them up or change them.

In the first half of the 20th century, Pennsylvania Railroad (PRR) was the largest publicly traded corporation in the world. By the second half, it was bankrupt. As freight and passenger traffic left the rails for the highways and airways, PRR continued to think of itself as being in the business of moving trains— not people or freight—from place to place. The idea of starting an airline would have meant giving up key assumptions about the "business we're in." So it defended its existing view of the business and battled the airlines for market share—a battle it couldn't possibly win. (Incidentally, airlines use a hub-and-spokes concept—in which all traffic moves along spokes connected to the hub at the center—which they borrowed from the railroads.)

The fast-food industry, which is explicitly designed to increase volume and reduce costs, is another great example. For most of the last quarter of the twentieth century, fast-food chains served enormous amounts of food quickly and cheaply by sourcing their ingredients from industrial suppliers, freezing the goods, and utilizing assembly-line production methods. The trade-off was that choice and freshness were quite limited. Then came the inevitable change in consumer tastes and preferences. The generation of Millennials and self-proclaimed foodies wanted fresh, organic, locally sourced ingredients and were willing to pay extra. Traditional fast-food chains were still doing a great business, but their *conceptual competencies* (i.e., concepts and practices they think are critical for success) of cheapness, convenience, and mass production were pretty much incompatible with the new emphasis on taste, freshness, and customization.[10]

This led to the rise of restaurants known in the trade as "fast-casual" (think Panera Bread, Shake Shack, Nando's chicken restaurants, and Chipotle Mexican Grill) that bridge the gap between fast-food outlets and full-service restaurants. The average check is more than 40 percent higher than that of traditional fast-food, and the "sustainable-food" approach is enjoying success across the world. In 2014, America alone, combined sales of fast-casual outlets rose by 10 percent, compared with six percent for fast-food chains. And Chipotle, previously owned by McDonalds, is now opening a new restaurant almost every other day and enjoying 20 percent annual growth.[11]

As these examples show, it's a mistake for any organization to believe that being successful at one point in time and staying on the same path will guarantee continued success. It's nearly impossible to capitalize on the opportunities brought about by changes in technology and consumer behavior by simply repeating what you've done before, no matter how successful you were. Although there's nothing wrong with maintaining the status quo when things are good, it's critical to understand that clinging to outdated concepts and practices makes it hard to change course when things (inevitably) go bad.

Conceptual Context:
Stopping People In Train Stations

In my lectures and classes, I often show a video from Improv Everywhere, a prank collective started by Charlie Todd that aims to disrupt the normal routines of everyday life to give people a positive, unexpected experience. To date, it has executed more than 100 public stunts involving tens of thousands of undercover "agents." In one case, Improv Everywhere focused on New York's Grand Central Station and asked the question: What do people expect will be happening at one of the world's busiest train terminals? Answer: Movement! So, being committed to disrupting normal routines, it decided to slow down the 500,000 or so people who rush through the station on a typical day. Charlie and his team organized 200 volunteers to synchronize their watches and freeze in place for 3 minutes at Grand Central's enormous main concourse. The reactions are hilarious as commuters and tourists talk to each other trying to figure out what's going on. One guy even removes a cell phone from a frozen woman's hand (and then puts it back). The scene that gets the most laughs is when a maintenance vehicle driver does his best to explain on a two-way radio why he has stopped on the concourse: "There's hundreds of people frozen everywhere. They're not moving. I... ah...I need some help."[12]

The reason I show audiences this video is that it's easy to imagine a typical business resembling the concourse at Grand Central. Everyone in the organization is busily running around, thinking of all the things they have to get done by the end of the day, the end of the week, the end of the month, the end of the quarter. But it's important for leaders to slow or stop an organization's short-term activities and provoke long-term thinking. Slowing down to "think" might happen once a year at the offsite retreat, but changes in thinking speed are conspicuously absent from day-to-day management. Why? Because slowing down is uncomfortable. Speed and efficiency within an organization is synonymous with decisiveness and productivity.

It's important for leaders to slow or stop an organization's short-term activities and provoke long-term thinking.

In the field of judgment and decision making, the researcher and author Daniel Kahneman describes the thinking speeds we use as a dual mode of fast and slow cognitive activities, which he labels System 1 and System 2.[13] The first is what we generally call intuition, and we often don't know that we're using it. Our decisions are effortless, unconscious, and fast. System 1 produces shortcuts that enable us to function rapidly and effectively. That's valuable but it can lead to errors. The second system is effortful, conscious, and slow but makes fewer mistakes. Most of our shortcomings in reasoning come from thinking quickly when we believe that we're thinking slowly. In other words, we use our slow thinking (System 2) to support a judgment that our fast thinking (System 1) already made.

At NYU Stern's Innovation Lab, where students conceive and execute disruptive business concepts, we refer to this tendency to think fast as the "first idea fallacy"—falling in love with the first plausible idea or explanation because of the gratification it brings and the decisiveness it demonstrates. Students and executives alike seem determined to reach a conclusion in their thinking as quickly as possible. It's as though the simple fact of thinking about something implies a lack of decisiveness and becomes an excuse for inaction.

The fallacy of first ideas arises when an apparently plausible solution is taken to be the "right" direction. Its "obviousness" seems to prove its validity. The problem is that satisfaction with the first idea effectively prevents any search for other ideas—many of which could be just as good or better. We come up with a usable idea that seems to solve a particular problem. And because we can't think of any other idea, we accept that first solution as the best one. The *only* one.

Of course, fast thinking isn't just modus operandi for people generating ideas—it's also built in to the process of evaluating those ideas. We have a tendency to deal with a new idea by selecting features that are similar to old ideas and trying to evaluate it within a *conceptual context* that we're already familiar with. Instead of trying to assess all the details and then decide how to react, whoever is evaluating a particular idea concentrates on the features that show that it fits within a particular context, or on features that show how it's different. When the idea is safely orientated, we know how to react to it by framing an initial either/or judgment[14] such as "This is great, it's the Warby Parker of [fill in the blank]," or "The industry leader, Luxottica tried that a couple of years ago and it didn't work." Sometimes we're mindful of these contexts and use them as shorthand to explain our intuition. At other times this method of judgment exerts its influence behind the scenes, below our level of conscious awareness.

The major trap here is that new ideas can't always be effectively judged on the basis of experience. Our faith in our own intuition makes us prone to error—especially when we're trying to predict the future from the context of the past or the present. Harvard professor Clayton Christensen, whose theory of disruptive innovation I described in the introduction of this book, discovered this bias in his own thinking after predicting in 2007 that Apple's iPhone wouldn't be successful: "The iPhone is a sustaining technology relative to Nokia. In other words, Apple is leaping ahead on the sustaining curve [by building a better phone]. But the prediction of the theory would be that Apple won't succeed with the iPhone. They've launched an innovation that the existing players in the industry are heavily motivated to beat: It's not [truly] disruptive. History speaks pretty loudly on that, that the probability of success is going to be limited."[15] The error in this prediction comes from the way it was initially framed, not from the way it was subsequently argued. As Christensen later acknowledged, "What I missed is that the smartphone was competing against the laptop disruptively. I framed it not as Apple is disrupting the laptop, but rather [the iPhone] is a sustaining innovation against Nokia. I just missed that."[16]

As this example shows, the frame of reference sets the context by telling us where to look and what to look for. The context can often be right, but only within the frame of reference we have *chosen* to use. And we usually—implicitly or explicitly—pick the most obvious one, the one that we've used before to evaluate similar ideas, and the one most closely aligned with our experience. The more we use a familiar frame of reference, the more confident we are in using it again, and the cycle repeats. As the popular saying goes, if the only tool you have is a hammer, everything looks like a nail.

Remember the pen I talked about in Chapter 6? I was making the point that the object itself doesn't have much value if you already have one or two. Now, let's go a step further. The value of that pen can change drastically depending on the context. When I was thinking of the pen only as a writing instrument, its value was limited. But what if I were being mugged in a dark alley? If I had that pen in my pocket, I might be able to stab my attacker and get away. In the context of a weapon—in the right circumstances—that pen is worth a lot. And what if I was a doctor in a remote location and someone near me collapsed and needed an emergency tracheotomy (there always seems to be a doctor on TV performing life-saving surgery with office supplies)? In the context of emergency medical equipment, that pen is incredibly valuable. The key to being a disruptive leader is to train yourself to look at the same idea from all sorts of different angles. Then you need to train your team to do the same.

The inability (or unwillingness) to look at things from different angles might explain how 15 venture capitalists dismissed the idea for Airbnb, the digital accommodations marketplace that people use to rent out their homes or spare rooms like a hotel. "I thought the idea was crazy," recalls Paul Graham, the cofounder of Y Combinator. "Are people really going to do this? I would never do this."[17] In fact, the only thing that saved the company was a cereal box. Design and technology writer Austin Carr describes how the startup came up with an idea to put the "breakfast" in what they were then calling AirBed and Breakfast.

They created two Airbnb-branded cereals, Obama O's and Cap'n McCain's, to sell online during the height of election fever. Airbnb found a small manufacturer who agreed to fabricate 1,000 cartons in exchange for a cut of the royalties. The team bought generic Cheerios and Chex, swapped the cereal into its own boxes, hot-glued the tops, and priced them at $40 each. The stunt worked. They received national media coverage and raised $30,000, enough to keep the company afloat until Paul Graham and Y Combinator came around and decided to invest.

Disruptive ideas like Airbnb will always be dismissed if we judge new ideas through the context of old ideas—at least until signs of the need for change are so obvious that we can't ignore them any longer. In a few short years, Airbnb became the poster child for what's now called the "sharing economy"—a concept that's changed the context for how we think about "owning" cars, parking spaces, boats, motorcycles, power tools, and other everyday items. We're now readily accepting rides from strangers (Lyft, Uber), eating food in their dining rooms (Feastly), and leaving our pets at their houses (DogVacay, Rover).[18] So it's easy to see how *wrong* an idea like renting out your home like a hotel appears in the old context of hotels having to "own" big pieces of real estate in order to be successful; and how *right* the idea appears in the new context of Airbnb becoming the world's largest hotel chain without owning a single property. One prominent Venture Capitalist, who passed on the initial pitch, now keeps a box of Obama O's in his office as a reminder of the mistaken (billion-dollar) judgment call.[19]

Warning: One of these days you're going to find yourself embracing an idea that you'd previously rejected. Don't feel bad when it happens—we all do it.

The Devil's Brew

It's also possible for an idea to be both right and wrong at the same time—with each judgment being logically supportable—depending on the context. A famous example is the If-By-Whiskey speech made in 1952 by a lawmaker from the U.S. state of Mississippi—Noah "Soggy" Sweat—on the subject of whether Mississippi should continue to prohibit or finally legalize alcoholic beverages. When asked how he felt about whiskey,[20] he replied:

> If when you say whiskey you mean the devil's brew, the poison scourge, the bloody monster, that defiles innocence, dethrones reason, destroys the home, creates misery and poverty, yea, literally takes the bread from the mouths of little children; if you mean the evil drink that topples the Christian man and woman from the pinnacle of righteous, gracious living into the bottomless pit of degradation, and despair, and shame and helplessness, and hopelessness, then certainly I am against it.

> But, if when you say whiskey you mean the oil of conversation, the philosophic wine, the ale that is consumed when good fellows get together, that puts a song in their hearts and laughter on their lips, and the warm glow of contentment in their eyes; if you mean Christmas cheer; if you mean the stimulating drink that puts the spring in the old gentleman's step on a frosty, crispy morning; if you mean the drink which enables a man to magnify his joy, and his happiness, and to forget, if only for a little while, life's great tragedies, and heartaches, and sorrows; if you mean that drink, the sale of which pours into our treasuries untold millions of dollars,

which are used to provide tender care for our little crippled children, our blind, our deaf, our dumb, our pitiful aged and infirm; to build highways and hospitals and schools, then certainly I am for it.

In both arguments, "whiskey" (i.e., the idea) is exactly the same—but the context has changed. Shifting the frame of reference from "devil's brew" to "oil of conversation" makes for a very different discussion about the merits of whiskey. And that's the point. The disruptive leader uses different frames of reference to introduce different conceptual contexts—real or imagined circumstances that help people think through all aspects of an idea and play with the potential benefits. Why is this important? Because initially, it's hard for us to *imagine* any (truly) disruptive idea being successful, and if we can't imagine something being successful, we're inclined to give it the thumbs down. We consciously or unconsciously direct our attention toward all the reasons why it *won't* work. In a recent article on Mashable, serial entrepreneur Michael Wolfe answered the question, "What are the most ridiculous startup ideas that eventually became successful?"[21]

> Another MySpace or Friendster, except several years late. We'll open it up only to a few thousand overworked, anti-social Ivy Leaguers. *Facebook.*
>
> We'll sell books online, even though users are still scared to use credit cards on the web. Their shipping costs will eat up any money they save. They'll do it for the convenience, even though they have to wait a week for the book. *Amazon.*
>
> We're building the world's 20th search engine at a time when most of the others have been

abandoned for being commoditized money losers. We'll strip out all of the ad-supported news and portal features so you won't be distracted from using the free search stuff. *Google.*

How about a professional social network, aimed at busy 30- and 40-somethings. They'll use it once every five years when they go job searching. *LinkedIn.*

It's like email, SMS or RSS. Except it does a lot less. It'll be used mostly by geeks at first, followed by Britney Spears and Charlie Sheen. *Twitter.*

Would you have invested in any of these? Looking back with 20-20 hindsight, of course you would have. But at the time? Doubtful.

In short: If you don't think much of an outlandishly improbable idea at first, change your frame of reference and think about it again. Ask yourself, what is the context that's controlling my reaction? Is it possible for my intuition to be both right and wrong at the same time? Under what circumstances is this idea valuable? Even if you believe the idea is never going to work, a change in context could help you see its strengths rather than its weaknesses. By not allowing yourself to immediately respond to the downside, you're forcing the upside to reveal itself. If that hard-to-imagine value becomes clear, interest will be there to explore the idea further and extract as much "innovation capital" from it as available (see Chapter 6). That idea will breed another idea.

One-Finger Typing

There are situations, of course, when it's important to make fast judgments, but there are also situations when it's better to make slow ones. Leading an organization in disruptive thinking requires the latter because generating ideas and making decisions more quickly and more efficiently isn't the issue—the goal is to get greater value from each decision you make and each idea you generate. Thinking slowly is simple but not an easy thing to do. It requires the self-control to consciously stop thinking fast. It feels like procrastination, an unwillingness to make a tough decision, and an excuse for not taking action. All in all, a total waste of time. But when you're thinking disruptively, wasting time is an offensive rather than defensive strategy. Sometimes, inefficiency and redundancy are pros, not cons.

Quentin Tarantino for example, can't type. The acclaimed screen writer and film director typed out the 165-page script for his movie *Inglourious Basterds* with one finger (the second finger on his right hand, to be exact). And it was important for him to do it that way. He explains: "You write, write, write with a pen and you always overwrite. But when you have to translate it to just one finger, a really strong editing process takes over. Basically, if you don't think this sh*t is the bomb, you're not going to spend time typing the final draft with one finger."[22]

When leaders reconsider the role of speed in thinking, they discover that slowing the organization down is like asking it to type with one finger. The extra effort required from thinking with one finger creates a conceptual "barricade" that interrupts the smooth flow of intuition and allows the organization to think about something that you—and everyone else—would have been unlikely to think about.

As with my students, what companies choose not to think about is as revealing as what they do. And when it comes to disruptive thinking, what they ignore matters as much as—or more than—what they pursue. That's why Microsoft didn't think of Google, why AT&T didn't think of Skype, Hilton didn't think of Airbnb, Blockbuster didn't think of Netflix (until it was too late), Luxottica didn't think of Warby Parker, and why General Motors didn't think to create Tesla Motors.

Too many leaders send a directive to their organizations that incremental change is safe and that disruptive change is fraught with danger, when in fact the opposite is true. When you start believing that your fundamental purpose is to alter your status quo, rather than preserve it, your motivation and mindset will start to change. You'll begin to see opportunities beyond what others have defined as limits. You'll begin to rethink who you are and what you might become. As a disruptive leader, it's up to you to make those transformative moments possible.

If you don't, no one else will.

An Instinct for Change:

Look Where No One Else Is Looking

> "If you believe human wants and needs are infinite, then there are infinite industries to be created, infinite businesses to be started, and infinite jobs to be done, and the only limiting factor is human imagination."
> —Marc Andreesen[1]

As we've seen in the disruptive thinking process, Little Miss Matched succeeded with a disruptive solution that challenged conventional sock-industry wisdom. Eventually, the solution made its way onto the feet of tens of thousands of young girls around the country. As marketing expert Seth Godin has said about the company:

> Instead of a strategy built around a consultant's vision of "utility" or a strategy built around cheap or a strategy built around excessive retail distribution and heavy advertising, they built their strategy around one girl saying to another girl, "Wanna see my socks?"[2]

So, what was the problem that the solution addressed? Well, there wasn't any problem—and that's exactly the point. Most people in business are trained to focus only on problems—things that don't work and need fixing. But, as I've shown in this process, that's not the only way. In fact, quite often, it's no way at all.

But, it's not just about following a process. This book represents a mindset—a rebellious instinct to discard old business clichés and remake the market landscape. An eagerness to deliberately target situations where the competition is complacent and the customer has been consistently overlooked or underserved. Richard Branson captures the essence of disruptive thinking when he says this:

> One has to passionately believe it is possible to change the industry, to turn it on its head, to make sure that it will never be the same again...[3]

The revolution is in full swing. The potential for reinvention is all around us, and it's an exciting time to be thinking about how to structure (or restructure) your business, your community, or your life in ways that create new value.

Enjoy the possibilities.

Endnotes

Preface

1 "Don't wait for a couple of guys…": Endorsement for the first edition of this book, Linda Tischler, Senior Editor, *Fast Company*, November, 2010.

2 "…movies and licensing deals expired": For a more detailed account, see James Surowiecki, "The Next Level," *The New Yorker*, October 18, 2010.

3 "…rebranding of the retail chain Pearle Vision": Max Chafkin, "Warby Parker Sees the Future of Retail," *Fast Company*, 2015

4 "…doing the work of crisis without the crisis": This sentiment was developed from two sources. Paul M. Romer said, "A crisis is a terrible thing to waste," in reference to the increasing competition that America faces from rapidly rising education levels in other countries. Roberto Mangaberia Unger wrote, "The task of the imagination will be to do the work of crisis without the crisis," in response to the financial crisis of 2008. See "Using the Crisis to Remake the Market," www.law.harvard.edu/faculty/unger/english/pdfs/UsingTheCrisis.pdf

Introduction

1 "You do not…what you do": Jerry Garcia quoted in, Warren Bennis and Patricia Ward Biederman, *Organizing Genius* (Basic Books; 1 edition, 1998), p. 19.

2 Disruptive technologies: Clayton M. Christensen, *The Innovator's Dilemma: When New Technologies Cause Great Firms to Fail* (Harvard Business Press, 1997). See also Clayton M. Christensen and Michael E. Raynor, *The Innovator's Solution: Creating and Sustaining Successful Growth* (Harvard Business Press, 2003).

3 "Industries are being built…in full swing": Seth Godin, Welcome to the frustration decade (and the decade of change), blog post, January 1, 2010.

4 "Mastery of design, empathy, play": Dan Pink, *A Whole New Mind: Why Right-Brainers Will Rule the Future* (Riverhead Trade; Rep Upd edition, 2006).

5 "The recipes we use": Paul Romer, An Interview with Paul M. Romer, *Strategy+Business*, November 20, 2001.

6 "Requiring consensus on one step before moving": For elaboration on this point see Ravi Chhatpar, "Innovate Faster by Melding Design and Strategy," *Harvard Business Review*, September 2007.

Chapter 1

1 "I love tackling lazy industries": Richard Branson, *Business Stripped Bare: Adventures of a Global Entrepreneur* (Virgin Books, 2009), p. 68

2 "Seeing things as they are": The original quote is, "You see things and you say, 'Why?' But I dream things that never were, and I say, 'Why not?'": George Bernard Shaw.

3 "Willing to test all hypotheses": Niall Ferguson quoted in, Robert S. Boynton, "Thinking the Unthinkable: A profile of Niall Ferguson," *The New Yorker*, April 12, 1999.

4 "A collective change of heart": Niall Ferguson, *Empire: The Rise and Demise of the British World Order and the Lessons for Global Power* (Basic Books, 2003).

5 "The key to the Allies' victory": Niall Ferguson, *The Pity Of War: Explaining World War I* (Basic Books, 1999).

6 "A surplus of similar companies": Jonas Ridderstrale and Kjell Nordstrom, *Funky Business: Talent Makes Capital Dance* (Bookhouse Publishing, 1999).

7 "The hero is not the murderer": Quentin Tarantino quoted in, Hermann Vaske, *Standing on the Shoulders of Giants: Hermann Vaske's Conversations with the Masters of Advertising* (Gestalten Verlag, 2001).

8 "Wii killed the idea that a video game": Joshua Cooper Ramo, *The Age of the Unthinkable: Why the New World Disorder Constantly Surprises Us And What We Can Do About It* (Little, Brown and Company, 2009), p. 125.

9 "Group together those with similar characteristics": For more detail on competitive audits see David A. Aaker, *Strategic Market Management* (Wiley; 9th edition, 2009).

10 "Scale up or scale down, move in the opposite direction, or completely do without": These methods are based on the "provocation" principle of lateral thinking developed by Edward de Bono. For more background see Edward de Bono, *Lateral Thinking: Creativity Step by Step* (Harper Colophon, 1973).

11 "I'm always trying to turn things upside down": Tibor Kalman interview with Charlie Rose, December, 1998.

12 "In its first year, the magazine's circulation": Susie Rushton, "How Monocle Survived its First Year," *The Independent London*, February 18, 2008.

13 "Think about the 'secret recipe'…in the restaurant business": Nassim Nicholas Taleb, *The Black Swan: The Impact of the Highly Improbable* (Random House, 2007).

14 "We have turned eating into an experience that": Ferran Adrià quote from Julia Hanna, "Customer Feedback Not on elBulli's Menu," HBS Case, November 18, 2009. For a detailed account of the El Bulli dining experience and their approach see Ferran Adrià, *A Day at El Bulli* (Phaidon Press Inc., 2008). El Bulli closed as a restaurant in 2011 and reopened as an educational institute and creativity center in 2014.

Chapter 2

1 "The most important advances are…": Sir Francis Bacon, Novum Organum (*Classic Reprint*, Forgotten Books, 2010).

2 "When people are looking at Macs…": Jonathan Ive, "Apple's Aesthetic Core," *Paper Magazine*, May 2002.

3 "…ethnographic or contextual research". The theory and practice of ethnographic research for design is rich and diverse. A detailed overview of its methods is beyond the scope of this book. For readers interested to know more, see Dev Patnaik, *Wired to Care: How Companies Prosper When They Create Widespread Empathy* (FT Press, 2009); Brenda Laurel, *Design Research: Methods and Perspectives* (The MIT Press, 2003); and Adam Richardson, *Innovation X: Why a Company's Toughest Problems Are Its Greatest Advantage* (Jossey-Bass; 2010).

4 "When the Quicken team came to my house": Intuit press release, August 01, 2005.

5 "Consumers told us…": Adam Chafe, "Dutch Boy Debuts New 'Twist & Pour' Paint Container," press release, June 11, 2002. See also, Julie Dunn, "Pouring Paint, Minus a Mess," *New York Times*, October 27, 2002.

6 "Global warming a problem?": Seth Godin, "Bear shaving," blog post, August 03, 2009.

7 "…the qualities we value have simply changed": Robert Capps, "The Good Enough Revolution: When Cheap and Simple Is Just Fine," *Wired Magazine*, August 24, 2009.

8 "Since its launch…": Case Study: Bank Of America, "How it Learned that What Customers Really Want is to Keep the Change," *Business Week*, June 19, 2006.

9 "People need help saving themselves…": Dan Heath and Chip Heath, "Why Customers Will Pay You to Restrain Them," *Fast Company*, April 1, 2009.

10 "…exercising is a should…:" Ibid.

11 "Because paper is a physical embodiment…": Abigail J. Sellen and Richard H. R. Harper, *The Myth of the Paperless Office* (The MIT Press, 2003).

12 "It's the story of a firefighter…": Jonah Lehrer, Annals of Science, "The Eureka Hunt," *The New Yorker*, July 28, 2008, p. 40.

13 The Flip video camera was discontinued in 2011 as an overall strategy to exit aspects of its consumer business. The Flip phone was still popular at the time of the shut down despite growing competition from smartphones.

14 "…an act of cognitive deliberation…": Ibid.

15 "How can it possibly work without water?": Gianfranco Zaccai, Insight, "Designed for Loving," *Business Week*, July 21, 2005.

16 "Here's how Continuum captured insights": Gabriella Lojacono and Gianfranco Zaccai, "The Evolution of the Design-Inspired Enterprise," *Rotman Magazine*, University of Toronto, Winter 2005.

17 Let's go through the same process with the Swiffer: This example has been adapted for the purpose of clarifying the framework outlined in this chapter. It is not intended to imply that Continuum documented the project using these terms or followed the process described. See www.dcontinuum.com for information on the Swiffer case study.

18 Work with a recruiter: Professional recruiters have large, proprietary databases of potential participants, and are often a necessity either because you're dealing with a market where you don't have a presence or you don't have the time and/or resources to handle it. Start by identifying recruiters that work in the target area, and get a quote. In the USA, estimate about $125–150 per recruit, and an additional $100–150 per hour as an incentive for each participant. Research facility rentals run approximately $500–$1,000 for a half day rental and $1,000–$1,500 for a full day rental. Remember to include prep and set-up time. If conducting research internationally, recruiting and incentives are not standard, so ask a local contact. Doing your own recruiting will always be more in terms of labor, but less in terms of expenses.

Chapter 3

1 "Imagination is more important…": Albert Einstein, quoted in "What Life Means to Einstein: An Interview by George Sylvester Viereck," *The Saturday Evening Post*, Vol. 202 (26 October, 1929), p. 117.

2 "Paralyzed by possibility": Beth Comstock, conversation with author.

3   For more information on blending together products, services, and information networks, see Stan Davis and Christopher Meyer, *Blur: The Speed of Change in the Connected Economy* (Grand Central Publishing; 1999).

4   "This bottle of wine…": Bruce Sterling, *Shaping Things* (The MIT Press, 2005).

5   "My relationship with this bottle…": Ibid.

6   It's always a good tactic to look for examples: There are many references to this tactic in the literature on creative thinking. For additional background see Edward De Bono, *Serious Creativity: Using the Power of Lateral Thinking to Create New Ideas* (Harper Business, 1993); and Michael Michalko, *Thinkertoys: A Handbook of Creative-Thinking Techniques* (Ten Speed Press; 2 edition, 2006).

7   "Cliche is the root of all…": Robert McKee, *Story: Substance, Structure, Style and The Principles of Screenwriting* (It Books, 1997).

8   "…the next great value breakthroughs…": Thomas L. Friedman, *The World Is Flat: A Brief History of the Twenty-first Century* (Farrar, Straus and Giroux; Expanded and Updated edition, 2006).

9   "Nintendo wondered if": For the extended story of the Wii's development, see Joshua Cooper Ramo, *The Age of the Unthinkable: Why the New World Disorder Constantly Surprises Us And What We Can Do About It* (Little, Brown and Company, 2009). See also Osamu Inoue and Paul Tuttle Starr, *Nintendo Magic: Winning the Videogame Wars* (Vertical, 2010).

10 "A lot of lavatory basins": Luke Williams, "The iPod and the Bathtub: Managing Perceptions through Design Language," *Design Mind*, Vol. 3, September 2005. Jonathan Ive's biography is available at www.designmuseum.org/design/jonathan ive.

11 "The freshness of an idea…": Marc Andreessen quoted in Richard Farson and Ralph Keyes, *Whoever Makes the Most Mistakes Wins* (Free Press, 2002).

12 "You'd feel that user focus…": Jason Kilar, interview with Charlie Rose, August 3, 2009.

13 "Can you imagine seeing a movie called…": Stephanie Palmer, *Good in a Room: How to Sell Yourself (and Your Ideas) and Win Over Any Audience* (Crown Business, 2008).

14 "…the tradeoffs that Pure Digital had to…": Robert Capps, "The Good Enough Revolution: When Cheap and Simple Is Just Fine," *Wired Magazine*, August 24, 2009.

15   For more information on visualizing systems, see Peter M. Senge, *The Fifth Discipline: The Art & Practice of The Learning Organization* (Crown Business; Revised edition, 2006).

16   "It's not enough to say…": Elizabeth Diller quoted in Justin Davidson, Our Local Correspondents, "The Illusionists," *The New Yorker*, May 14, 2007, p. 128.

Chapter 4

1   "Your company's chance of creating…": Gary Hamel, *Leading the Revolution: How to Thrive in Turbulent Times by Making Innovation a Way of Life* (Harvard Business Press; Revised Edition, 2002).

2   "One of the biggest corporate blunders": Peter Carlson, "The Flop Heard Round the World," *The Washington Post*, September 4, 2007.

3   "Run them through the following": These activities were developed and refined by Jason Severs of frog design, New York.

4   "It was the exact opposite": Malcolm Gladwell, *Blink: The Power of Thinking Without Thinking* (Little, Brown and Company, 2005).

5   "It looks as though it came from…": Ibid.

6   "The problem market research…": Ibid.

7   "The value of prototypes…:" Michael Schrage, *Serious Play: How the World's Best Companies Simulate to Innovate* (Harvard Business Press, 1999).

8   "Creating a dialogue between…:" Ibid.

9   "On April 11, 1970, the Apollo 13 Mission…:" Adapted from William Lidwell, Kritina Holden, and Jill Butler, *Universal Principles of Design* (Rockport Publishers, 2003), p. 171. For a dramatized film version of these events see Ron Howard's, *Apollo 13*, Universal Pictures and Imagine Entertainment, 1995.

10   "…a character in a marketplace narrative": Michael Schrage, *Serious Play: How the World's Best Companies Simulate to Innovate* (Harvard Business Press, 1999).

11   "Include close-ups of details where needed": For more detail on storyboarding techniques see Karen Holtzblatt, Jessamyn Burns Wendell, and Shelley Wood, *Rapid Contextual Design: A How-to Guide to Key Techniques for User-Centered Design* (Morgan Kaufmann; illustrated edition, 2004).

12   "This is a quick and dirty reel": To understand the look and feel of quick video prototypes see the student work of the HCI Group (Human Computer Interaction) at Stanford University, California (www.hci.stanford.edu). There are many examples online. Search Google Video for "stanford video prototypes."

Chapter 5

1 "I opened the script and it exploded...": Christoph Waltz quoted in, "At War with Quentin Tarantino," *Esquire UK*, September 2009.

2 "There are only three rules...": Somerset Maugham reportedly said this in response to a student's question while lecturing in a friend's English class.

3 "The problem is that the term 'elevator pitch'": Stephanie Palmer, *Good in a Room: How to Sell Yourself (and Your Ideas) and Win Over Any Audience* (Crown Business, 2008).

4 In the discussion time after the pitch, be prepared to explain the tradeoff between cost and benefits associated with implementation, dive into issues of technical feasibility, and make suggestions for how the solution can be further tested. If the pitch resonates with your audience, the next step is the development of a business case and profit model.

5 "Flow state": For more detail on the concept of "flow" and how it relates to attention see Mihály Csíkszentmihályi, *Creativity: Flow and the Psychology of Discovery and Invention* (Harper Perennial, 1997).

6 "... your ability to create a compelling introduction": John Medina, *Brain Rules: 12 Principles for Surviving and Thriving at Work, Home, and School* (Pear Press; Reprint edition, 2009).

7 Allen Brady & Marsh's pitch to British Rail: Jon Steel, "Pitching New Business," influx interview (influxinsights.com/blog/article/1034/read.do), November 14, 2006.

8 "Give the audience a hint of a scene." Orson Welles, U.S. filmmaker, actor, producer quoted in Frank Brady, *Citizen Welles: A Biography of Orson Welles*, ch. 8 (Anchor, 1990).

9 "The cat sat on the dog's mat": Sean Hall, *This Means This, This Means That: A User's Guide to Semiotics* (Laurence King Publishers, 2007).

10 "Will the sheriff kill the shark...": Robert McKee, *Story: Substance, Structure, Style and The Principles of Screenwriting* (It Books, 1997).

11 "*Alien* is *Jaws* on a spaceship": All three examples from Chip Heath and Dan Heath, *Made to Stick: Why Some Ideas Survive and Others Die* (Random House, 1 edition, 2007).

12 "The compact, five-word phrase...": Ibid.

13 "The answer lies in the 'early adopters'": For further information on capturing an "early market" see Alex Wipperfurth, *Brand Hijack: Marketing Without Marketing*, ch. 14 (Portfolio Trade, 2006).

14 "They combined the three things...": Seth Godin, *Unleashing the Ideavirus* (Hyperion, 2001).

15 "Revolutionary goals, but evolutionary steps": Gary Hamel, *Leading the Revolution: How to Thrive in Turbulent Times by Making Innovation a Way of Life* (Harvard Business Press; Revised Edition, 2002).

16 "…'Just Do It' was not about sneakers…": Scott Bedbury and Stephen Fenichell, *A New Brand World: Eight Principles for Achieving Brand Leadership in the Twenty-First Century* (Penguin, 2003).

Chapter 6

1 "We have a good ability…": Larry Page quoted in Steven Levy, "Why Moon Shots Matter," *Wired*, January 17, 2013.

2 "…disrupt the disrupters": Adapted from Stanley Bing's amusing take on the business world's obsession with disruption, "Enter the Disrupters," Fortune, July 25, 2013.

3 "…growth springs from better recipes…": Paul M. Romer, "Economic Growth," *The Concise Encyclopedia of Economics*, www.econlib.org/library/Enc1/EconomicGrowth.html. For the original source, see Paul M. Romer, "Endogenous Technological Change," University of Chicago, pages.stern.nyu.edu/~promer/Endogenous.pdf

4 "…the world of intangible ideas is not." For more information and a great summary of the theory, see Matt Ridley, "The Rational Optimist: How Prosperity Evolves," (*Harper Perennial*; Reprint edition, June 7, 2011).

5 "Cooking up ingredients in a kitchen…": There are many references to this metaphor for innovation in addition to Paul M. Romer. See Edward De Bono, *Lateral Thinking: Creativity Step by Step* (Harper Colophon, 1973), and Matt Ridley, "The Rational Optimist: How Prosperity Evolves," (*Harper Perennial*; Reprint edition, June 7, 2011).

6 "In a widely cited example…": Adapted from Walter Isaacson's article, "The Real Leadership Lessons of Steve Jobs," *Harvard Business Review*, April 2012.

7 "…stifles thinking that challenges it": For this account of the Flyknit shoe and the quote from Mark Parker, see Austin Carr, "Nike: For a Pair of Revolutionary New Products and Culture of True Believers," The World's 50 Most Innovative Companies, *Fast Company*, March, 2013.

8 "…the only thing being risked…": For more information on managing risk through thinking, experimentation, and innovation portfolios, see Gary Hamel, *Leading the Revolution*, Plume; Reprint edition (July 30, 2002). See also Edward De Bono, *Lateral Thinking: Creativity Step by Step* (Harper Colophon, 1973).

9 "The breadth of its innovation capital…": For a full list check out, David Lidsky, "Most Innovative Companies in business," *Fast Company*, March 2014.

10 "…things that are not just incremental": Larry Page quoted in Steven Levy, "Why Moon Shots Matter," *Wired*, January 17, 2013.

11 "More than half of all startups…": "Entrepreneurs anonymous," *The Economist*, September 20th, 2014.

12 "Do you really want to be like Steve Jobs?": Ben Austen, cover story, *Wired*, August 2012.

13 "The art of talking trash": Max Chafkin, "The One-Two Punch," *Fast Company*, March 2014.

14 "…the biggest crock…": Ibid.

Chapter 7

1 "Are people really going to do this?": Paul Graham quoted in, Austin Carr, "Most Innovative Companies," *Fast Company*, March 2012.

2 "They're holding the horses": Adapted from Elting E. Morison, "Gunfire at Sea," *Men, Machines and Modern Times* (Cambridge, MA: MIT Press, 1966).

3 "…antilock brakes on automobiles": Adapted from William Lidwell, Kritina Holden, and Jill Butler, *Universal Principles of Design* (Rockport Publishers, 2003), p. 130-131.

4 "…they shape our thinking…": For a more detailed account of mental models, see Peter M. Senge, *The Fifth Discipline: The Art & Practice of The Learning Organization* (Crown Business; Revised edition, 2006).

5 "It's difficult to get someone to understand something…": Original quote is from American author, Upton Sinclair. Referenced in *Candidate for Governor: And How I Got Licked* (University of California Press, 1994), p. 109.

6 "At its peak, the company employed 21,000 people": For a detailed account of this example and an excellent analysis of the Polaroid story, see Andrea Nagy Smith, "What Was Polaroid Thinking," *Yale Insights*, November 2009. See also, Nick Bilton, "Innovation Isn't Easy, Especially Midstream," *New York Times*, April 15, 2012.

7 "…the company filed for bankruptcy": Ibid.

8 "We knew we needed to change the fan belt…": Ibid.

9 "This tendency to reconstruct the past…": For a good explanation of hindsight bias, see Michael Shermer, *The Believing Brain*, Times Books; 1st edition (May 24, 2011).

10 "…new emphasis on taste…": For a detailed account of the rise of fast casual restaurants, see James Surowiecki, "The Shake Shack Economy," *The New Yorker*, January 26, 2015.

11 "…enjoying 20 percent annual growth": "Fast-casual restaurants,"
    The Economist, January 10, 2015.
12 "They're not moving. I need some help": Quote from "Grand
    Central Freeze" video, Improv Everywhere, http://improvevery-
    where.com
13 System 1 and System 2": Daniel Kahneman, *Thinking, Fast and
    Slow* (Farrar, Straus and Giroux; 1 edition, October 25, 2011).
14 The use of analogies and contexts to frame judgements and influ-
    ence decision making is well-documented. The seminal work
    is perhaps, "The Framing of Decisions and the Psychology of
    Choice," Amos Tversky and Daniel Kahneman, *Science* 1981, vol.
    211, p. 453-458. Edward de Bono refers to this method of judgment
    as "polarization," in *Lateral Thinking: Creativity Step by Step*
    (Harper Colophon, 1973). See also, Scott Plous, *The Psychology of
    Judgment and Decision Making* (McGraw Hill, 1993), and Douglas
    Hofstadter and Emmanuel Sander, *Surfaces and Essences:
    Analogy as the Fuel and Fire of Thinking* (Basic Books, April 23,
    2013).
15 "…probability of success is going to be limited": Clayton
    Christensen interviewed by Jena McGregor, *Bloomberg
    Businessweek*, June 11, 2007.
16 "I just missed that": Ibid.
17 "I would never do this": Paul Graham quote and Airbnb-branded
    cereal story from Austin Carr, "Most Innovative Companies," *Fast
    Company*, March 2012.
18 "We're now readily accepting rides from strangers…": For an
    insightful account of the impact of the "sharing economy" on con-
    sumer behavior, see Jason Tanz, "Trust Us" cover story, *Wired*,
    May 2014.
19 "…reminder of the mistaken judgment call": Austin Carr, "Most
    Innovative Companies," *Fast Company*, March 2012.
20 "When asked how he felt about whiskey…": For an analysis of the
    speech, see William Safire, *Safire's Political Dictionary* (Oxford
    University Press; Revised edition, March 31, 2008).
21 "What are the most ridiculous startup ideas…": Michael Wolfe, "18
    successful startups that seemed crazy at first," *Mashable* via Quora,
    November 3, 2014.
22 "…typing the final draft with one finger": Quentin Tarantino quoted
    in, "At War with Quentin Tarantino," *Esquire UK*, September 2009.

Epilogue

1   "If you believe human wants and needs are infinite...": Marc
    Andreessen quoted in Thomas L. Friedman, *The World Is Flat: A
    Brief History of the Twenty-first Century*, (Farrar, Straus and
    Giroux; Expanded and Updated edition, 2006), p. 231.
2   "Wanna see my socks?": Seth Godin, "The power of remarkable,"
    blog post, June 18, 2008.
3   "One has to passionately believe...": Richard Branson, "The Money
    Programme," BBC, July 1998.

Acknowledgments

The initial spark for this book was generated when Michele Tepper put me in touch with Martha Cooley. The project was made possible by the vision, enthusiasm, and publishing support of Tim Moore, Amy Neidlinger, and Stewart Emery. Thank you all.

The creative community at frog design has provided an incredible home for the development of the thinking in this book. Special thanks to Valerie Casey, Ravi Chhatpar, Robert Curtis, Hartmut Esslinger, Robert Fabricant, Mark Gauger, Mikal Greaves, Chris Green, J Grossen, Jon Guerra, Cyrus Ipaktchi, Mike Lavigne, Tim Leberecht, Willy Loor, Doreen Lorenzo, Kristina Loring, Sara Munday, Howard Nuk, Mark Olson, Samir Patel, Mark Prommel, Adam Richardson, Patricia Roller, Mark Rolston, Christian Schluender, Jason Severs, Shady Shahid, Kate Swann, Michael Voege, and Carsten Wierwille. Prior to frog design, I worked with an inspiring cast of people in Australia who encouraged my interest in disruptive innovation: David Armstrong, Don Barbour, Greg Barclay, Julian Ditchburn, James Duncan, Bernard Heaphy, Roslyn Herbert, Murray Hine, Liz Hutchinson, Susan MacDonald, Jacqueline Moth, Sam Pearson, Greg Ridder, Peter Robinson, John Scholten, Patrick Shing, and David Teller.

The opportunity to join the faculty at NYU Stern School of Business was made possible by Scott Galloway, and the generous support of Adam Brandenburger and Peter Henry. For two years, I had the privilege of teaching this course with Peter Golder, who had a tremendous impact on the course curriculum and content. Thanks also to my amazing team at the

W.R. Berkley Innovation Lab (formerly the Berkley Center for Entrepreneurship): Jerllin Cheng, Cynthia Franklin, Patricia Miller, Loretta Poole, as well as our namesake and friend, Bill Berkley. To my students in the "Innovation & Design" course, a big thank you for helping refine the framework, clarifying the steps, and showing me how to talk about innovation without the consulting jargon.

The team at Pearson Education has been a pleasure to work with: Kristy Hart, Gloria Schurick, and Dan Uhrig. Thanks to Russ Hall for working his magic on the early drafts, and Lori Lyons for her astonishing patience and attention to detail on the final drafts. Special thanks to my superb editor, Jeanne Glasser Levine, for shepherding the manuscript through the writing process and shaping the book's final form.

A huge thank you to my literary agent, Jim Levine, for helping navigate the process—from proposal to print. Jim, your guidance and advice have been invaluable. Thanks also to the wonderful team at the Levine Greenberg Agency for their support—particularly Elizabeth Fisher and Kerry Sparks.

I'm indebted to my closest collaborator on this project, Armin Brott, who shaped and massaged the tone, language, and structure of this book with patience, insight, and unwavering commitment. Thanks also to my friend and former frog design colleague, Jonah Staw, for graciously sharing the story of Little Miss Matched and providing valuable insights on the development and positioning of this book.

To the superb writers, critical thinkers, and leaders who endorsed this book. You are a constant source of inspiration: Warren Berger, Jamyn Edis, Stewart Emery, Scott Galloway, Seth Godin, Peter Golder, Stuart Hogue, Martin Lindstrom, Ric Peralta, Cordell

Ratzlaff, David Rogers, Andy Stefanovich, Linda Tischler, and Bill Wackermann. This book exists because of the intellectual foundation laid by Edward de Bono, Gary Hamel, and Tom Peters.

And finally, a heartfelt thank-you to my friends for your patient support: Tim Bilham, Paul Bryan, Simon Chard, Rod Cobain, Katarina Cobain, Anya Emerson, Felicity Forrester, Jason Humphris, Pete Jones, Jackie Laws, Toby MacKelden, Kirsten MacKelden, Ingrid Mallia, Matt Rainsford, and Tamzine Walshe. Thanks to Richard Troy for expert feedback on book jacket concepts; Damian Kernahan for insights on the manuscript; and Ainslie Baker for accommodating me during writing spurts in London. Special thanks to Ben Baker for generously providing the author photo, and Freddy Anzures for original cover design and Michael Graziolo for the updated version. I'm deeply grateful for the wonderful support of Natalie Kresen as well as the encouragement of my family: Grandfather, Lawrie (the original disruptive thinker), my parents, Jenny and Keith, and sister, Bri.

In memory of my uncle, Graeme Griffiths (1950–2015).

About the Author

LUKE WILLIAMS is an international authority in disruptive thinking, and in the practice of innovation as a leadership capability. He holds a faculty appointment at New York University's Leonard N. Stern School of Business, where he is Executive Director of Entrepreneurship and Founder of the W.R. Berkley Innovation Lab. As Clinical Associate Professor of Marketing at NYU, he teaches one of the most popular electives for business students in both New York and Shanghai.

Williams is the inventor of 30+ U.S. patents and has designed more than 100 products in industries ranging from transportation to finance, and healthcare to consumer electronics. He is a fellow at frog design, one of the world's most influential product strategy and design firms. His instruction on innovation has been sought by many of the world's largest corporations and most agile startups.

Williams has addressed the UN General Assembly on the future of entrepreneurship; facilitated innovation workshops for the World Economic Forum; lectured in 21 countries, and has been featured in media ranging from *Bloomberg BusinessWeek* and *Fast Company* to *The Wall Street Journal*.

Beyond the Book

At some time, someone somewhere is going to disrupt your entire industry. Shouldn't it be you?

Luke Williams shows you how to cultivate a culture of disruptive thinking and leadership through his engaging lecture topics and course offerings:

- **Disruptive Thinking: Sparking Business Transformation with Innovation** (Keynote Speech)

    Disruptive Thinking is about fostering a culture of innovation leadership that provides the framework and motivation to generate disruptive strategies and execute unexpected solutions. It is an essential skill for any business leader, from a small start-up to a global corporation, with the desire to transform organizational processes and behaviors, and ask, "Why hadn't we ever thought about our business and culture this way before?"

- **Disruptive Leadership: Fostering a Culture of Game-Changing Innovation** (2-Day Course with NYU Stern School of Business)

    The scale of the challenges we face and the accelerating speed of innovation demands a new approach to innovation leadership—a new way of fostering counterintuitive ideas, forcing improbable insights, and opening minds to uncomfortable solutions.

To achieve these objectives, the course combines presentations and discussion with practical exercises where participants apply disruptive leadership principles to business issues and scenarios. This program is eligible for Continuing Professional Education Credits (CPE).

To inquire about open enrollment or customized professional education courses, contact the NYU Stern Executive Education office at +1 (212) 998-0789 or ExecEd@stern.nyu.edu.

To inquire about speaking engagements, workshops, or seminars, contact Washington Speakers Bureau at +1 (703) 684-0555 or info@washingtonspeakers.com.

You can find a full profile and video footage of Luke Williams at www.washingtonspeakers.com/LWilliams.

Index

Symbols

7-Eleven, 153
20-20 hindsight, 211

A

Adria, Ferran, 37-38
Aeron chair, 123-125
Airbnb, 219-220, 224
Allen Brady & Marsh, 151
Amazon, 222
analogies in pitches, 160-162
Andreesen, Marc, 91, 227
angina drug example, 63
antilock brakes, 207-208
Apollo 13 moon mission, 128-129
Apple, xii
  awareness versus consumer
    research, 41-42, 85
  design decisions, 89-91
  iPhone, 218
Applied Imagination, 82
assumptions, as best practices, 212-214
AT&T, 224
Avon, 190
awareness, consumer research versus,
  41-42

B

Bacon, Sir Francis, 41
Bank of America, 53
bear shaving, 51
Bedbury, Scott, 167
best practices, 212-214
Bezos, Jeff, 195
BlackBerry, 96
*Black Swan, The: The Impact of the
  Highly Improbable*, 36
blending ideas, 92-96, 104, 178
Blink, 123
Blockbuster, x, 54, 224
Blumenthal, Neil, xiii
Bowerman, Bill, 146
brainstorming
  focusing creative effort, 86-88,
    177-178
  forcing connections, 88-92
  lack of focus, 82
Branson, Richard, 19, 228
British Rail, 151, 154
Build a Bear, 169
bundles, 93
businesses
  clichés
    *disrupting by denying, 31-32,
      37*
    *disrupting by inverting, 30-31,
      36*

inertia tension points, 53

Inglourious Basterds, 143, 224

innovation

capital for, 191-195

conceptual innovation

best practices, 212-214

frames of reference, 217-223

mental models, 206-211

mindset, 201-205

speed of thinking, 214-217, 223-225

for growth, 186-188

personalities of disruptive leaders, 195-198

recipes for, 189-191

Innovator's Dilemma, The, 3

insight

from observations, 60-63, 176

asking why, 63-65

capturing, 65-66

describing opportunities, 70-72

generating into opportunities, 67, 75-76, 177

moving to opportunities, 67-70, 76-77

providing, 155-157

insight board, 56-58

Instagram, 209-211

interaction clichés, 28

intercept observations, 47-48, 74

interview teams, 54-55

intuition, 216

intuitive nature of idea, providing, 160-162

Intuit's "Follow Me Home" program, 46

inversion, disrupting clichés, 30-31, 36

investments in innovation, 191-195

iPhone, xii, 83, 218

iPod, 91, 99

Isaacson, Walter, 195

isolated approaches

blending ideas, 92-96, 178

holistic approaches versus, 82-84

iteration cycles, 129-130

Ive, Jonathan, 42, 91

J–K

Jaws, 19, 157

JC Penney, 169

Jobs, Steve, xii, 190, 195

Kahneman, Daniel, 216

Kahn, Louis, 47

Kalman, Tibor, 31

Keep the Change program, 53

Kilar, Jason, 94

Kodak, 101, 209-211

Kounios, John, 63

L

labeling product, 98

LaVigne, Mike, 51

Legere, John, 196

Levie, Aaron, 196

Linens 'n Things, 169

LinkedIn, 27, 222

Little Miss Matched, 19, 34, 227

disruptive hypotheses, 35, 72

pitching disruptive solutions, 168-169

target customer feedback, 137-138

transforming opportunities into ideas, 102-103

Luxottica, xiii, 224

M

Macy's, 169

Made to Stick, 161

Mann Gulch fire, 60-61

market research. *See* contextual research

Marsh, Peter, 151

Maugham, W. Somerset, 145

McDonald's, 153

McKee, Robert, 88, 157

memory mapping, 116-118, 138, 179

mental models, 206-211

Merthyr Tydfil, Wales, 63

MGM, 97

Microsoft, 224

Microsoft's Xbox, 25

Milkman, Katherine, 54

mindset of disruptive leaders, 201-205

mock-ups, 134-135, 140, 181

Monocle, 33

motivation for change, providing, 164-166

motivation of disruptive leaders, 186-188

Mountain Dew, 27

MP3 effect, 52

Musk, Elon, 195-196

must-have customers, 45

Myth of the Paperless Office, The, 57

N

naming products, 96

Napster, 166

Netflix, xi-xii, 19, 224

New Growth Theory, 187, 191

New York Times, 89

New Yorker magazine, 60

Nike, 146, 167-168, 190-191

Nintendo's Wii, 25-26, 89-90

Nokia, 190, 218

noninvasive observations, 47, 74

Nordstrom, 137

Nordström, Kjell, 24

NYC Taxi and Limousine Commission, xii

O

observations, 44-46, 175-176

coding, 59-60

insights, 60-63, 176

asking why, 63-65

capturing, 65-66

describing opportunities, 70-72

generating into opportunities, 67, 75-76, 177

moving to opportunities, 67-70, 76-77

intercept, 47-48, 74

interview teams, 54-55

noninvasive, 47, 74

organizing into themes, 56-59, 75-76

pain points, 48-49

planning and gathering, 73-74

pre-arranged, open-ended interview with, 46-47, 73

recording, 56

tension points, 50

inertia, 53

shoulds versus wants, 54

value, 51-53

workarounds, 50-51

open discussions, 122-125, 139

opportunities

describing, 70-72

generating from insights, 67, 75-76, 177

ideas

blending together, 92-96, 104, 178

documenting, 96-102, 105, 179

focusing creative efforts, 86-88, 177-178

forcing connections, 88-92

refining, 93-96

moving from insights to, 67-70, 76-77

transforming into ideas, 104

stumbling blocks, 81-85

S

saccharin, 89

Salk Institute, 47

scaling, disrupting clichés, 33, 37

Schrage, Michael, 126

Seinfeld, 32

selecting ideas, 125-126, 180

Sellen, Abigail, 57

Serious Play, 126

Shaping Things, 83

sharing economy, 220

Shaw, George Bernard, 20

Shopping Express, 193

shoulds versus wants tension points, 54

Simpsons, The, 123

skincare and personal-health devices, 110

Skype, 224

Sony, 100-101

Sony's Playstation, 25

Speed, 161

speed of thinking, 214-217, 223-225

Starbucks, 153, 168

status quo, demonstrating, 153

Staw, Jonah, 34-35, 72, 102-103, 137-138, 168-169

Sterling, Bruce, 83

storyboards, 132-133, 139-140, 180

stumbling blocks

  overcoming

    blending ideas, 92-96, 178

    documenting ideas, 96-102, 179

    forcing connections, 88-92

    maintaining focus, 85-88, 177-178

  transforming opportunities into ideas, 81-82

    isolated versus holistic approaches, 82-84

    lack of documentation for ideas, 84-85

    lack of focus, 82

subscription-premium model, 33

Sweat, Noah "Soggy," 221

Sweet'N Low, 89

Swiffer brand, 64

T

Taleb, Nassim Nicholas, 36

Tarantino, Quentin, 24-25, 97, 143, 224

target consumers, feedback, 110-116, 179

  group rankings, 119-121, 139, 180

  improvement exercises, 121-122, 139, 180

  individual rankings, 118-119, 139, 179

  memory mapping, 116-118, 138, 179

  open discussions, 122-125, 139, 180

Teletouch gearshift, 111

tension, building, 154-162, 170, 182

tension points, 50

  inertia, 53

  shoulds versus wants, 54

  value, 51-53

  workarounds, 50-51

Tesla Motors, 224

themes

  organizing contextual research, 56-59

  organizing observations, 75-76

thinking. *See* conceptual innovation; ideas

This Means This, This Means That, 154

Thurman, Uma, 25

Tiffany & Co., 190

Time magazine, 100 Most Influential People, 22

Tischler, Linda, x

T-Mobile, 196

Todd, Charlie, 214-215

Toys R Us, 169

traditional hypotheses, disruptive hypotheses versus, 20-22

turning points, providing, 157-160

TV remote control design, 45

Twist & Pour paint containers, 49-50

Twitter, 27, 223

U–V

Uber, xii

Under Armor, 96

unreasonable provocation, reasonable prediction versus, 20

value tension points, 51-53

Vanity Fair magazine, 54

Viagra, 64

video cameras, "feature creep," 62

video gaming industry, clichés in, 25-26

videos of ideas, 135-136, 140-141, 181

visualization, 101

Volvo, 161

W

Walt Disney Entertainment Company, 79-81, 94

Waltz, Christoph, 143

wants versus shoulds tension points, 54

Warby Parker, xiii, 224

waterless cleaning products, 64

Weeks, Wendell, 190

Welles, Orson, 152

whiskey speech, 221-222

Wii (Nintendo), 25-26, 89-90

Wired magazine, 52, 195

Without Limits, 146

Wolfe, Michael, 222

workaround tension points, 50-51

X–Y–Z

Xbox (Microsoft), 25

Y Combinator, 219-220

Zipcar, 31